D1713352

Faith and Sanctification

BOOKS BY G. C. BERKOUWER

MODERN UNCERTAINTY AND CHRISTIAN FAITH

THE TRIUMPH OF GRACE IN THE
    THEOLOGY OF KARL BARTH

STUDIES IN DOGMATICS SERIES —

THE PROVIDENCE OF GOD

FAITH AND SANCTIFICATION

FAITH AND JUSTIFICATION

FAITH AND PERSEVERANCE

THE PERSON OF CHRIST

GENERAL REVELATION

DIVINE ELECTION

MAN: THE IMAGE OF GOD

THE WORK OF CHRIST

Studies in Dogmatics

Faith and Sanctification

BY

G. C. BERKOUWER

PROFESSOR OF SYSTEMATIC THEOLOGY
FREE UNIVERSITY OF AMSTERDAM

Wm. B. Eerdmans Publishing Company
Grand Rapids, Michigan

Translated by John Vriend

from the Dutch edition, *Geloof en Heiliging*
published by J. H. Kok N. V., Kampen, The Netherlands

Seventh printing, January 1980

ISBN 0-8028-3028-5

PHOTOLITHOPRINTED BY EERDMANS PRINTING COMPANY
GRAND RAPIDS, MICHIGAN, UNITED STATES OF AMERICA

Contents

Timeliness and Relevance

CHAPTER I

Timeliness and Relevance

S HOULD anyone select for special study the relation between faith and justification, as we have done in a previous book, he could by no means avoid the present, equally relevant study of the relation between faith and sanctification. This new problem thrusts itself upon our attention with such immediacy that we scarcely realize we are stepping onto new ground. The history of the church and of theology, at any rate, throws into sharp relief the dove-tailed interconnection between justification and sanctification. Engage in controversy concerning the one, and presently you are talking about the other. In this controversy one accuses the other of allowing justification to be assimilated by sanctification, only to be told that he, on the other hand, through his preoccupation with justification, crowds out sanctification. It is no wonder at all that in our time, ever since justification returned to the arena of theological debate, sanctification was at its heels.

In any discussion about sanctification it is evident that we are concerned, not with a maze of theoretical abstractions, but with the bread-and-butter problems of this life. One can even say that a discussion about sanctification is the more relevant because also the unbeliever evinces interest in what the church professes in the matter. For he detects in this teaching a presumptuous note, the pretension, namely, of being saintly, of being different. And, of course, this pretension seems to the accuser entirely unwarranted.

The confession that the believer is justified by faith alone seems not to interest the unbeliever; the pretension of being

9

different so much the more.   Here at least is room for scrutiny, a chance to put Christianity on trial.   Is this sanctification indeed a radiant reality crowding out the darkness?   Are
the children of God indeed a different breed from the rest of
men?   Or is sanctification a mere fancy, beautiful but barren
when put to the test?   The believer can, of course, shrug off
these questions and say that the unsanctified can never in his
life understand the true significance of sanctification.   Be that
as it may, but he had better remind himself that the Scriptures
are very emphatic about the connection between good works
and the scrutiny of the world.   One of the aims of the church
in this world, according to Paul, is "that ye may become
blameless and harmless, children of God without blemish in
the midst of a crooked and perverse generation, among whom
ye are seen as lights in the world" (Phil. 2:15).

The Church of Jesus Christ is not a self-contained unit, in
complete isolation from and unlinked with the rest of the
world, but stands in a determinate, God-willed relationship to
it.   In the prophecy of Zechariah we are told that "it shall
come to pass that ten men shall take hold, out of all the lan-
guages of the nations, they shall take hold of the skirt of him
that is a Jew, saying, We will go with you, for *we have heard*
that God is with you" (Zech. 8:23).   Not only do the Scriptures speak of the spread of salvation in terms of hearing, but
also in terms of seeing: "Ye are the light of the world.   A city
set on a hill cannot be hid. . . . Even so let your light shine
before men: that they may see your good works, and glorify
your Father who is in heaven" (Matt. 5:14, 16).

This revealed impossibility — the impossibility of creeping
under a bushel — gives to our discussion, and to all discussion
of sanctification, an existential relevance.

There is, of course, the possibility of misinterpreting the
impossibility of seclusion.   The Pharisees, who had their own
way of avoiding seclusion, did not thereby escape the condemnation of Christ.   To them he proclaimed the value of privacy:

"Take heed that ye do not your righteousness before men, to be seen of them" (Matt. 6:1-14). This word of warning does not, however, destroy the force of his teaching concerning good works as shining light. It is exactly this relation between required hiddenness and impossible hiddenness which gives to any discussion of sanctification its peculiar character. To say that "Jesus restores to piety its long-lost modesty when he directs it into the inner chamber,"[1] is to condemn the "theatrical nature of the pharisaic practice of piety,"[2] but it certainly does not forever keep his followers from contact with this world. Those who are sensitive to the danger of publicized piety will understand also why a lamp cannot be put under a bushel or bed but must be put on a lampstand. "For there is nothing hid, save that it should be manifested; neither was anything made secret, but that it should come to light" (Mark 4:21-23). This is not a self-contradictory teaching but a revelation, full of meaning and admonition, of two aspects of the sanctified life.

*   *   *

The timeliness of our subject becomes the more evident when we observe to what extent the problem of the renewal of life is attracting the attention of moralists. Amid numberless chaotic and demoralizing forces is sounded, as if for the last time, the cry for help and healing, for the re-organization of a dislocated world. The therapy prescribed may be varied, the call for moral and spiritual re-armament is uniformly insistent.

Also, in the interest of what seems to be a common goal, namely the renovation of society and resistance against its deterioration, there are the efforts of those who wish to unite humanistic with Christian ideals. We may have divergent

---

1. Kittel, *Theologisch Wörterbuch zum Neuen Testament,* III, compare krupto, page 975.
2. *Ibid.,* page 977.

views on the nature of morality, they say, but is there no common sphere of operation in which to work toward the "sanctified" society? Surely concrete results are more important than the rationale that produced them. Could we not somehow acquire a common vision of the Good?

These are the questions we must answer. For implicit in them is the intent to destroy the connection between justification and sanctification, as well as the bond between faith and sanctification. It may seem that by insisting on these bonds as vital to the Christian life we are withdrawing from full participation in the world of everyday affairs. But the man who understands the relation between faith and sanctity knows better; he knows that he can pave his way into real life only by keeping these connections intact. We need the rationale of the Christian faith also if we would understand the sanctity that makes recruits for that faith. We need it to understand Peter when he talks about proper conduct among the Gentiles, "that, wherein they speak against you as evil-doers, they may by your good works, which they behold, glorify God in the day of visitation" (I Peter 2:12).

Although the sanctity that is out to make recruits may never be immune from the dangers of becoming theatrical, these dangers are not overcome by a denial of the rationale involved. Our only safeguard is to keep the muscles of sanctity attached to the tendons of our faith.

Only thus will it be apparent that sanctification embraces all of life. Without this connection, sanctification would have to operate in a void. Sanctification, if it is to be at all, must not take place merely on some underground level of psychic life, quite in defiance of all outside disturbances, but must be the redemptive touch of our faith on all of life. The sanctity that is at work on the leash of faith cannot lead us — or mislead us — away from concrete realities; for faith makes all of life meaningful and draws us out of ourselves. This relationship, this connection, is the subject on which we would reflect in succeeding chapters.

* * *

As with the problems of justification, so with those of sanctification, the stage is set and the discussion, to a degree, determined by dialectical theology. When this new theology began to speak again, and with great emphasis, about the justification of the ungodly as God's sovereign verdict of acquittal, a verdict by no means precipitated by the moral condition of the acquitted, it was natural to ask what place would be assigned by this theology to sanctification. A widely-voiced fear was that sanctification would be absorbed by the act of justification and that, on this view, the distinction between the two was hardly warranted. In Holland a striking change took place in theological discussion. Whereas before 1920 the question was always whether ethical theology allowed room for forensic justification, after that the problem of the reality of sanctification came to the fore. Again the relation between justification became the subject of more than tepid discussion. Involved in this discussion were various problems relative to Christian activities such as Christian politics. In this debate the dilemma of "theatrical versus Christian sanctification" was again thrust to the surface. Pharisaism, the distinction between the church and the world, solidarity in guilt — all this was fodder for the religious press. Varied decisions were made in this period and it became clearer than ever that dogmatic reflection, far from being abstract speculation, is an activity immediately relevant to, and richly productive for, practical life. And the heart of the problem was, in almost every instance, the nature and reality of sanctification.

The Reformation issue is as alive today as it was four hundred years ago; and we know that any discussion concerning justification by faith alone has direct bearings on sanctification. Karl Barth has been accused by numerous Catholic theologians of an extravagant emphasis on the "sola-fide" doctrine, in which he would be pushing the Reformation doctrines to their logical extremes. In his theology the justification of the ungodly, it was alleged, is an "unreal" divine verdict and human life passes between the poles of God's judgment and God's grace without undergoing any alteration whatever.

The Catholic polemic against Sola-fide took place in a period in which especially Newman was revived. Remarkably enough, the debate concerning sanctification was dominated by memories of two nineteenth-century men, namely, Newman and Kohlbrugge. Now it seems we must accept the dilemma of having either a passion for real and tangible holiness or Christ as our sanctity and He alone. The sound and fury of the discussion, far from signifying nothing, indicate how little there is here of sterile theory.

To understand the Sola-fide of the Reformation as the only proper response to the bibical message of sovereign grace is to know that this Sola-fide can never be a threat to real sanctification. Such a threat can emerge only from a denial or devaluation of this doctrine. The ancient feud of Rome with the Sola-fide doctrine, based as it is on the view that Sola-fide is subversive of sanctification, must be called Rome's most fundamental error. It was no other than Sola-fide which made clear the true significance of sanctification, and distinguished it from all moralistic effort at self-improvement, in short, from all practices and beliefs which do violence to Sola-fide and, therefore, to Sola-gratia.

"Sola Fide" and Sanctification

CHAPTER II

"Sola Fide" and Sanctification

ONE WHO has pondered the far-reaching significance of the "sola-fide" doctrine — justification by faith alone — is immediately faced with the question whether this cardinal concept does not make all further discussion superfluous. Can anything be added, one might ask, to the joy of a man who has heard the voice of God saying "Not guilty!", who has seen the doors of his prison cell open, not in the wishful dreams of the night but amid the full reality of salvation? Does not the chalice of joy already overflow with the exclamation: The Lord has delivered us "out of the power of darkness. and translated us into the kingdom of the Son of his love; in whom we have our redemption, the forgiveness of our sins"? (Col. 1:13-14).

Does not every addition — to posit a few questions — weaken the radical nature of grace, emasculate our creed which declares: "But what does it profit you now that you believe all this? That I am righteous in Christ before God, and an heir to eternal life."?[1] Antinomianism may be a dangerous heresy, but is it not true that it had its origin in the Gospel and intended at least to be a reminder of what lies behind us, the truly finished work of Christ, the all-sufficient atonement which defies addition? "For ye died, and your life *is* hid with Christ in God" (Col. 3:3). What then of the customary distinction between justification and sanctification? Is not this distinction an undeniable, though perhaps unconscious, devaluation of the "sola-fide" doctrine? And are the tensions

---

1. *Heidelberg Catechism*, Lord's Day 23.

created by the charges, tossed to and fro among theologians, of over-emphasis on either justification or sanctification, to be traced perhaps to a basic error in this distinction?

In order to answer these questions it is necessary, first of all, to assert that we wish, not to evade the sovereignty of divine grace, but at the same time to do justice to the testimony of the Scriptures. Always, in response to the Scriptural message, students have felt the necessity of distinguishing between these doctrines and, further, of inquiring into the relation between them. For it is undeniably true that this distinction is rooted in the Scriptures.

The epistles of Paul will serve as an example. The apostle has spoken emphatically of justification by faith without the works of the law and has declared that the purpose of God with regard to election stands "not of works, but of him that calleth" (Rom. 9:11); in the same epistle, however, and apparently without sensing any intolerable tension or antinomy, he entreats his fellow-believers to present their bodies "a living sacrifice, holy, acceptable to God" (Rom. 12:1). Elsewhere he exhorts them to perfect their holiness in the fear of the Lord and to cleanse themselves from all defilement of flesh and spirit (II Cor. 7:1). And in these admonitions he does not confine himself to woolly, indefinite appeals but states, with clarity and concreteness, what he wishes: Unity of spirit (Rom. 15:6), and mutual recognition and reponse (Rom. 15:7), wisdom in that which is good (Rom. 16:19), a fleeing from fornication (I Cor. 6:18); and he points out that in the daily life of the believers the fruits of the Spirit are these: Love, joy, peace, longsuffering, kindness, goodness, faithfulness, meekness, self-control (Gal. 5:22). The life of the believer, whether he be in Galatia or elsewhere, must be easily distinguishable from that dominated by the fruits of the flesh: Fornication, uncleanness, lasciviousness, idolatry, sorcery, enmities, strife, jealousies, wraths, factions, divisions, parties, envyings, drunkenness, revellings, and such like (Gal. 5:19 ff).

This Pauline insistence on sanctity, moreover, has the unqualified support of the other apostles. They warn against a dead faith (James 2:14), the unbridled tongue (James 1:26), neglect of the poor (James 2), and hatred (I John 3:15). And these warnings go hand in hand with the admonition to love one another, not only in word, neither with the tongue, but in deed and truth (I John 3:18), and to practice self-purification (I John 3:3). Nor must these things be thought secondary and unimportant. The writer to the Hebrews distils the essence of all these admonitions into this one — and it sounds menacing: "Follow after peace . . . and the sanctification . . . without which no man shall see the Lord." (Heb. 12:14). In the tense eschatological atmosphere of John's Revelation one may read, above the gate to the New Jerusalem, this inscription: "Without are the dogs, and sorcerers, and the fornicators, and the murderers, and the idolators, and everyone that loveth and maketh a lie" (Rev. 22:15; cf. Rev. 22:11).

Everywhere in the Scriptures one may hear the trumpet-sound of this clear and forceful imperative: "For this is the will of God, even your sanctification" (I Thess. 4:3).

The evidence is so compelling that one is inclined to ask why there should have been so much discussion on the subject. As compared with the complications which later ignited conflict, are not the Scriptural pronouncements on sanctification simple and non-problematic? Nonetheless it would be a mistake to dismiss all later discussions as senseless. For too often men have talked about the command to be holy in such a way as to mutilate the biblical message. It is certainly not enough for a man to say that he honors the law of God and for that reason strives toward holiness. The people of Israel offer proof that one may live in the climate of absolute imperatives and still perish. It is therefore of the utmost importance, not only to acknowledge the *fact* of the Scriptural command to be holy, but especially to understand the *nature* of this command.

Although the imperative here spoken of is anything but an independent factor serving to complete our salvation, it must be said emphatically to be in some way or other connected with our salvation. The apostle Paul preaches holiness with repetitive fervor, but in no way does he compromise his unequivocal declaration: "For I determined not to know anything among you, save Jesus Christ, and him crucified." (1 Cor. 2:2). Not for a moment would he do violence to the implications of that confession. Hence in his every exhortation he must be relating his teaching to the cross of Christ. From this center all lines radiate outward — into the life of cities and villages, of men and women, of Jews and Gentiles, into families, youth, and old age, into conflict and disaffection, into immorality and drunkenness.

If we would keep this center, as well as the softer and harder lines flowing from it, in true perspective, we must be thoroughly aware that in shifting from justification to sanctification we are not withdrawing from the sphere of faith. We are not here concerned with a transition from theory to practice. It is not as if we should proceed from a faith in justification to the realities of sanctification; for we might as truly speak of the reality of justification and our faith in sanctification.

Indeed, nearly all the problems of sanctification are bound up with the question of this "transition" from justification to sanctification. One of the complaints which assail us constantly is that sanctification is being cut loose, or abstracted, from justification. And if it be true that a wedge has been driven between them, the church is certainly in mortal danger of slipping into moralism, with its attendant self-conscious pride or its nagging uncertainties.

The moment sanctification is ejected from the temple of faith, and hence of justification, that moment justification by faith has become an initial stage on the pilgrim's journey, a supply-station which later becomes a pleasant memory. Successive stages would follow, that of sanctification for instance, and in this stage it would be up to man to act. Understood in this fashion, the distinction between justification and sanctification would amount to assigning the one act wholly to God and the other wholly to man. Sanctification would then be described as a series of devout acts and works performed by the previously justified man. The distinction between justification and sanctification could then be traced to the subject of each act: God or man. So an obvious division would have taken place; man — this would be our conclusion — is not called upon to justify but to purify himself.

It is not hard to see that the Scriptures are intolerant of this division. We are told, for example, that Christ "was made unto us wisdom from God, and righteousness and *sanctification,* and redemption" (I Cor. 1:30), and about man as an object of divine sanctification we hear: ". . . but ye were sanctified, but ye were justified in the name of the Lord Jesus Christ, and in the Spirit of our God" (I Cor. 6:11). The believers "are sanctified in Christ Jesus" (I Cor. 1:2; cf. Acts 20:32; 26:18); the benediction in the epistle to the Thessalonians reads: "And the God of peace himself sanctify you wholly, and may your spirit and soul and body be preserved entire, without blame at the coming of our Lord Jesus Christ" (I Thess. 5:23).

When in view of the approaching return of Christ the Revelation of John comes to the congregation with the final challenge: "He that is unrighteous, let him do unrighteousness still: and he that is filthy, let him be made filthy still," it immediately adds a positive note to this utterance: ". . . and he that is righteous, let him do righteousness still: and he that is holy, let him be made holy still" (Rev. 22:11). Certainly this is a strong call to action, but it is also clear that this action can never be an independent human function but is related, in a unique way, to the divine act of sanctification of which the Scriptures speak. The denial of this truth is the error signalized by Bavinck when he wrote: "Many indeed acknowledge that we are justified by the righteousness of Christ, but seem to think that — at least they act as if — they must be sanctified by a holiness they themselves have acquired."[2] This view he rejects as being in conflict with the testimony of the apostles, and he sees in it the return to the bondage of the law. Bavinck does not mean to say, of course, that one may never speak of the activity, the self-purification, of believers. For that he can point confidently to the testimony of the Scriptures, but he is trying to define what he calls "evangelical sanctification," which "is as different from that of the law as the righteousness of faith is from that acquired by the works of the law."[3]

It may be said that all discussions on this subject are concerned with this "evangelical sanctification," that is, with the question how sanctification is related to the gospel message, the glad tidings of salvation.

*   *   *

A variety of pronunciamentos has suggested the idea that we have here an antinomy. On the one hand sanctification was spoken of as an act and gift of God, on the other as an act and obligation of the believer. Abraham Kuyper spoke of this "being sanctified and yet to be sanctified" as "the puzzling, but indispensable contradistinction which the Lord himself wove into the fabric of his Kingdom."[4]

---

2. *Gereformeerde Dogmatiek*, IV, page 233.
3. *Ibid.*, page 233.
4. *Uit Het Woord*, First Series I, "Heiliging," page 195.

Taken strictly, such talk of an antinomy or contrast is objectionable.[5]   For of such *unreconciled* juxtaposition the Scriptures know nothing.   As is evident already in the Old Testament, the holiness of God's people is not a moral quality which arises from their own actions and achievements, but it is rooted in the sanctifying action of God.   Even though we may not carelessly identify the words "holy" and "to sanctify" as used in the Old Testament with the same words as used in the New Testament, yet in the Old Testament also this twofold aspect is found in striking contiguity.   Consider this appeal from Leviticus: *"Sanctify yourselves* therefore, and be ye holy; for I am Jehovah your God.   And ye shall keep my statutes, and do them: *I am Jehovah your God who sanctifieth you"* (Lev. 20:7, 8).   God himself had chosen his people Israel and separated it, made it a holy people.   This separation did not, in any sense, rest on Israel's moral strength or piety, but had its foundation solely in divine election.   Nor is this sanctification only of temporary significance; on the contrary, when God commands his people to be holy, that is, to keep his commandments, he introduces — no, not a new element in the relation between him and his people, but rather an appeal to them to become and to remain conscious of the sanctity with which he has sanctified them, and to walk and live accordingly.   That is the sanctification of Israel, and therefore there can be no talk of an antinomy.   Quite in harmony with this appeal, too, is the word of the Lord which came to Ezekiel: "And I will put my Spirit within you, and cause you to walk in my statutes, and ye shall keep my ordinances and do them" (Ezek. 36:27; compare verses 25, 26).

Failing to understand this unity, Israel failed also to understand its own sanctification.   It lost sight of the indissoluble

5. *Ibid.*, page 198: "Nevertheless we believe we may assert also with regard to these sayings that they have basically the same signification."   He points to John 13: "Here too we find the dictum, 'Ye are clean,' set side by side though *unreconciled* with the *seeming* contradiction, 'If I wash thee not, thou hast no part with me.'"   (Note the italicized words!)

connection expressed in the following: "For I am Jehovah your God: sanctify yourselves therefore, and be ye holy; for I am holy" (Lev. 11:44; compare Lev. 19:2). Immediately following this command comes its ground: "For I am Jehovah that brought you up out of the land of Egypt, to be your God: ye shall therefore be holy, for I am holy" (Lev. 11:45). This interconnection between God's holiness, his sanctification of Israel, and Israel's self-sanctification is fundamental: so fundamental, in fact, that the apostle Peter applies this utterance to the obedient children of the New Testament church who stand in the grace brought to them at the revelation of Jesus Christ (I Peter 1:15, 16). In the Old Testament, as later, the recurrent motif in the admonition to fear one's parents, to keep the Sabbath, and to flee from idols, is the holiness of God: "I am Jehovah your God" (Lev. 19 –– the entire chapter). At the end of a long series of admonitions in Leviticus 19 comes the clinching summary: "And ye shall observe all my statutes, and all mine ordinances, and do them: I am Jehovah" (Verse 37).

Hence the relation between God's sanctification of Israel and its self-sanctification is not one of competition or even of cooperation. Nor is the obedience of Israel a return service, a payment in kind, by which it may, to some extent, bring about its own redemption. On the contrary, every summons is an expression of the sanctifying act of God, of his sovereign arrangements for the separation of his people. Behind this separation lies his gracious election, his love, his oath which he swore to the fathers. Therefore Jehovah brought them out of Pharaoh's hand with a strong arm and . . . "therefore keep the commandment, and the statutes, and the ordinances, which I command thee this day, to do them" (Deuteronomy 7:7-11).

At this point we observe the distinctiveness of Israel's existence. Other Gods are excluded because HE is the Lord. Since Israel was chosen and sanctified to be the people of God.

therefore it had no other task than to live *as* the people of God. The command, "Be ye holy, for I am holy," has rightly been called the epitome of the entire Old Testament revelation. The foundation of Israel' life, of all its manifestations, and hence of every admonition, is this belonging to God. This admonition, far from being at variance with the sanctifying act of God, rests upon it. Changing the words of Kuyper, "being sanctified and, yet, to be sanctified," to "being sanctified and *therefore* to be sanctified," one would express a basic idea of the Old and New Testament. The sanctification initiated by God has, one might say, "self-evident" consequences. On every occasion and in every sector of its existence Israel must give expression to the unique relationship established by God. From this vantage-point one may understand the opposition to the false prophets who deceptively taught it to follow and serve other gods: "Ye shall walk after Jehovah your God, and fear *him,* and keep *his* commandments, and obey *his* voice, and ye shall serve *him* and cleave unto *him*" (Deut. 13:1-4).

The Scriptures abound with references to this harmonious correlation. It is the pulse-beat of every admonition. Without it the relation between justification and sanctification cannot be understood. The apostles also know and preach this "self-evident" sanctification. People have wondered about the commandments of the New Testament and asked themselves whether the church of Christ has been brought back under the law after all and whether Jesus Christ was perhaps a new Lawgiver in disguise. Does it seem more palatable, perhaps, if we say that now the believer may, but is not compelled to, be obedient?

Elsewhere we shall inquire into the relation between sanctification and the law, but one thing is entirely certain, namely, that in the New Testament all admonition is grounded in and proceeds from the mercy of God. To those who would make of sin and grace a matter of trifling calculation and who would continue in sin that grace might abound — over against these

Paul cries out: "We who died to sin, how shall we any longer live therein?" (Rom. 6:1). *That* is the rationale of Paul's admonition, its stimulus, and urgency. With a view to the immorality threatening the church Paul asks whether they do not know that their bodies are members of Christ (I Cor. 6:15) and a temple of the Holy Spirit (I Cor. 6:19). Sharply he demands: "Do you know that you are not your own?" "For ye were bought with a price: glorify God therefore in your body" (I Cor. 6:19, 20).

Hence it is not true that believers are children of God — justified, purified, sanctified, called, and loved — without having to heed the voice of admonition. This antinomian error not only denies the true sanctification of believers but has lost sight of the holiness of God and his sanctifying influence. Because it is God who sanctifies, this admonition is fully integral with the Gospel of grace. The children of light are called upon to walk as children of light (Eph. 5:8) and because Christ has made us free, we must stand fast in our freedom (Gal. 5:1; compare Col. 3:1-3). For this reason it is not mere sophistry to take exception to the word "antinomy." Basic to this word is the conception that God's sanctification and the self-sanctification of the believer are two equipoised, mutually limiting magnitudes. But the Scriptures are averse to such equivalence. The sanctification there demanded is always an implicate of the sanctification that originates in God's mercy. Hence the sanctification of believers is never an independent area of human activity. The supposed antinomy is supplanted by the idea, clearly advanced in the Scriptures, that the sanctification of the believer is a corollary of his faith.

Nothing, it is true, need or can be added to the salvation we have in Christ Jesus. The grace of God is truly abundant. The believers who have received this abundance of grace and the gift of righteousness now stand in a new relation to God. Once they were darkness and now they are children of light — light in the Lord (Eph. 5:8).

For this reason the Scriptures are full of the call to action: believers, bestir yourselves! Only a completely perverted exegesis can assert the contrary. Christian activity is certainly not to be excluded, or belittled, or condemned: but if this activity is to be sound it must never be severed from its relation to the mercy of God.

* * *

The significance of the "sola-fide" doctrine for our subject is becoming apparent. This Scriptural insight into the true meaning of admonition suffered eclipse again and again throughout the history of the church. Having mutilated the "sola-fide" doctrine, people would then fall back on a *cooperative* relation between divine grace and human action. This mutilation is especially prevalent in the Roman Catholic doctrine which teaches that justification must be understood as the infusion of supernatural grace. On this basis, sanctification can have meaning only as the successive development, with the cooperation of a free will, of the grace implanted. Justification and sanctification are brought down on the same plane, while their interrelation becomes nowhere clearly visible.

Sanctification, on these terms, takes place in an atmosphere of forces and counter-forces, among which faith may then perform its now very modest function of preparing for justification; and justification itself becomes almost indistinguishable from sanctification. Once the sanctifying grace takes root, many forces throw in their weight. The cultivation of the grace received, after its initial infusion, is then the essence of sanctification. In this process the sacraments must, of course, play their part.

And so Catholicism assigned to sanctification a qualitatively different content from that indicated by the Reformers. For the Reformers saw the way of salvation primarily under the aspect of God's gracious disposition in Christ Jesus, under the aspect of unmerited forgiveness. The "sola-fide" of justifica-

tion made it possible, once for all, to regard justification and
sanctification as almost identical acts of God, operative, in con-
centric circles of increasing radius, on the plane of individual
human life. This *dunamis*-conception does principial violence
to the correlation between human faith and divine grace —
not because it points to the power of God but because, in the
stress and tension of multiple forces, it deflects·faith from its
true bearings on divine grace. And no subsequent re-emphasis
on the divine initiative in redemption can repair the damage.

In opposition to this hypothetical field of forces, the Reformation again restored sanctification in its true relation to
faith. The immediate consequence of the "sola-fide" doctrine
was exactly this indissoluble bond between faith and sanctification. And we speak of faith, not as a point of departure for
a fresh emission of power, or as a human function or potency
producing other effects, but of faith as true orientation toward
the grace of God and as the life which flourishes on this divine
grace, on the forgiveness of sins.

It is almost incomprehensible, in view of all this, that
Catholicism should have understood the Reformation to say
that this forgiveness of sins, this acquittal and justification,
has no significance for the actual situation of the sinner: as if
the forgiveness of sins should cover the sinner with the gar-
ment of Christ's righteousness without affecting the body un-
derneath. The Reformation was understood to keep redemption forever in the realm of objectivities, in the world of faith,
the righteousness of Christ, and the promise. A verdict of
exoneration would come to man but, apart from receiving the
function of faith with which to accept this strange verdict, he
underwent no real change.

The thesis that the "sola-fide" doctrine is averse to the renewal of life has often been pinned on the views of Luther.
The idea was that Luther had constructed his doctrine of justification by faith alone because of an inner conflict. He simply could not — so the story ran — overcome the burning

lusts of the flesh, and so he needed a view of salvation which would kindly release him from the guilt, though not from the corruption, of sin. Even after his justification man could not but sin because — Luther allegedly taught — human nature is not merely injured but utterly perverted, and divine grace does not restore man but brings him forgiveness and tells him all is "well" again.

To anyone who has had a whiff of Luther's writings this conception is incredible. Even a scanty initiation is enough to be convinced that justification for Luther meant much more than an external event with no importance for the inner man. Amid the stress of his reformatory polemics Luther wrote his "Concerning Good Works" in which he makes his position clear: "In this way I have, as I said, always praised faith, and rejected all works which are done without such faith, in order thereby to lead men from the false, pretentious, pharasaic, unbelieving good works, with which all monastic houses, churches, homes, low and higher classes are overfilled, and lead them to the true, genuine, thoroughly good, believing works."[6]

Against the *meritoriousness* of good works Luther indeed directed a fierce polemic; but in all his opposition he was fully conscious that Christ must assume form in the believer,[7] and he treats extensively of the significance of the ten commandments for the life of the believer. One may well ask how people came so shamelessly to distort his teaching and to ascribe to him this purely "external" view of faith, when he himself on numerous occasions affirms the inner restoration of believers.

This distortion can be explained only by saying that men went on to misconceive the "sola-fide" doctrine. They frequently interpreted it to mean *"in* faith alone" and detected in it a contrast between faith and reality, faith and works, faith and sanctification. They saw in faith as it were a desiccated

6. *Works of Martin Luther,* The Philadelphia Edition, Vol. I, page 193.
7. *Ibid.,* page 203; compare Galatians 4:19.

technique corresponding to an external, imputative justification and placed over against that the inescapable reality of sanctifying grace. They polemicized constantly with an appeal to the words of Paul that "the love of God hath been shed abroad in our hearts through the Holy Spirit" (Rom. 5:5) and adduced, as clear Scriptural doctrine, the idea that we are "really made just."[8]

Actual justification as distinguished from the "merely" declaratory justification: that, in brief, is the Catholic antithesis. Gerard Brom regards the "sola-fide" doctrine, with its exclusive "sola," as absolutism, and says in this connection, "Luther thought he could glorify the Almighty with an attitude of complete inaction." He accuses the Reformer of reading into the Bible a faith without love and even of asserting that the Bible neither demands service nor proclaims any commandments. Again it is faith *versus* reality, love, and good works.

The cardinal difference between Catholicism and the Reformation, according to Dr. Van de Pol, lies in their respective views of reality. Says he, " . . .according to Catholic doctrine, the true Revelation is a revelation of reality, whereas, according to the Reformation, it is a revelation of the Word."[9] He does not mean, of course, that the Reformed proclamation of the Word would have no bearings on reality. On the contrary, this proclamation, since it is concerned with the incarnation, reconciliation with God, and eternal life, definitely treats of reality. Yet there is a radical difference. "For according to the Reformation the believer enjoys the possession of this reality only by faith."[10] The Reformation viewed the work of redemption as a reality of the past and the fulfilment of God's promises as a reality of the future. Now the believer lives

---

8. W. H. Van de Pol, *Het Christelijk Dilemma*, 1948, page 155.

9. *Ibid.*, page 207ff.

10. *Ibid.*, page 209.

"by faith" and not by sight. He lives "between the times" and is related to the realities of the past and future by faith alone. Van de Pol admits that this "alone" does not detract from the reality he is discussing, but asserts that Catholicism is concerned with a reality which is much different and more profound, namely, "a new supernatural reality which broke into the world of space and time through revelation." This reality the Reformation does not acknowledge. It recognizes only the limited reality which is known by faith alone.

In connection with this characterization of the cardinal difference, Van de Pol was criticized to the effect that his orientation was too emphatically Barthian ("between the times"), and that by the contradistinction of "Word" and "Reality" he virtually called in question or even denied the genuineness and reality of the fellowship which the Reformed believer has with his Lord. In reply, Van de Pol re-emphasizes that the Reformation is also concerned with reality. On the Reformed view one may, in fact, speak of reality in five ways. First there is the reality of the divine decree, then the reality of relation to God, a historical reality (the redemption history), a new reality in heaven (the risen and glorified Christ), and finally the promised reality of future bliss. Our faith is definitely focussed on a reality in each of these five ways. And so he does not at all call in doubt the genuineness of the religious life led by his Reformed brethren. There is, he says, no absolute contrast between a revelation of the Word and one of Reality. But Rome teaches still another reality, not acknowledged by the Reformation, a mystical reality of a higher order, not belonging to perceptual reality but nonetheless so integrated with the visible as to be present and operative in it. It is the supernatural reality of Christ's sacramental presence on the altar, at Mass, in the Church as his body, in Holy Baptism, and other sacraments which infuse into the soul, and maintain in it, the grace that is a form of supernatural, divine Life.

With the addition of all these restrictions, it would seemingly have been better to concentrate the discussion on the supernatural, mystical reality just mentioned.   It was this reality, indeed, on which the Reformation split with Rome. From this point of view we can approach the controversy of the Reformation — an approach to be preferred to that of Brom who starts with the idea that the "sola-fide" is antithetic to love, to the reality of the sanctified life.   Far from making the "by faith alone" exclusive, in the sense explained, the Reformation made it fundamental.   Faith was to be the foundation of what they called the "new obedience."   Even the most perfunctory inspection of Reformation writings brings this out vividly.

In 1520 Luther wrote about good works and Christian liberty, but nowhere does he, on the basis of the "sola-fide," justify libertinism.   In discussing the tenth commandment, he does say that no man is free from evil lusts, let him try what he will; and that, in trying to be rid of them, he will learn to seek his aid elsewhere so that he may be free indeed and so that the commandment, which he cannot obey, may be fulfilled by another.   But this looking for aid beyond himself has nothing to do with an external, ineffective imputation.   The Other from whom he sought his salvation, remains of absolute significance for the life of the believer, and the Christian liberty thus created is anything but a permit to be idle or to do evil.

The point at stake is the reality of the "by faith alone," a reality which accords with the dictum of John: "But as many as received him, to them gave he the right to become children of God, even to them that believe on his name" (John 1:12). Faith is not opposed to life but rather determines it and shoots meaning into it.   For this faith is focussed on grace — compare "sola fide" and "sola gratia" — and how could grace and pardon be without significance for actual life?   Faith is not a competitor of love and good works but rather a sponsor, and gives foundation to them because it acknowledges the grace of

God. Again and again, and for this reason, Luther pointed out the deep significance of the first commandment and accounted all works performed outside its sphere as nothing.

According to Luther faith precedes good works, good works follow faith. Whoever would invert that order speaks a "dark and dangerous language." For to him only the works as such would be important. Good works do not make a man good, says Luther, but the good and devout person must be there before the works. Of the reality of the new life there is no doubt, but Luther would place it in true biblical perspective. All-important for him is this new "being" implied in reconciliation and adoption. This is the reality from which springs faith. The adoption to sons — that is the foundation of sanctification, the *only* foundation. It is true that, for Luther, "being antecedes action."

The Sola-fide is at the heart of justification but no less at that of sanctification.

This becomes apparent when Luther argues emphatically from faith to love of one's neighbor: all one's works must promote the welfare of one's neighbor, since in his faith each has all the possession he requires and can therefore freely and lovingly devote his entire life to the service of his fellowman.

Thus the Reformer spoke, at a time when his life hung from a silk thread (1520), at a time when the Reformation was bitterly accused of libertinian tendencies. Thus these words — they have been called the most remarkable in Luther's writings — gave form to the significance of faith for life and made apparent in what sense faith is to be exclusive. One who so understands faith will continue to view the bond between faith and sanctification — given in the adoption to sons- as a legacy of the Reformation.

*   *   *

An interesting sidelight on the inveterate misrepresentation of the Reformed doctrine of justification is afforded by a passage in one of Luther's letters to Melanchthon. Roman polemicists have discovered in it final proof of Luther's libertinism and antinomianism. We are referring to the words. "Sin bravely!"[11] These words were the occasion of a furious diatribe aimed at Luther. Here was undeniable proof, at long last, of the subversive nature of the Reformed view of justification. A clear example of Catholic interpretation is found in Möhler. He cites Luther's words and says that "they may not be urged too strongly on account of the obvious spiritual exhaustion of the author," but in the history of dogma they remain important: "Sin bravely, but be even braver in the faith and rejoice in Christ who is the victor of sin and death and the world." Luther's words become even more suspect when we read the rest of the quotation: "Sin we must as long as we live. It is enough that through the riches of the glory of God we know the Lamb who takes away the sins of the world. From that Lamb no sin can separate us, though we should fornicate a thousand times a day or commit murder."[12] In this connection Möhler reminds us of another word of Luther: "If adultery could be committed in the faith it would not be a sin."[13]

Involved in this dispute are two questions. First, was Luther justified in speaking as he did? We need, also with respect to the words of Luther, to maintain a certain amount of critical reserve. It seems to us that Luther might have been more cautious. In an overheated theological atmosphere we should strive for intelligible formulations. This is the more evident when we consider the disgrace of Antinomianism falsely associated with the Reformation.

Another question is whether Luther intended in these daring words to throw the door open to libertinism. It is quite apparent that this cannot be the case. He does not intend,

---

11. The words are: "Esto peccator et pecca *fortiter,* sed fortius fide et gaude in Christo, qui victor est peccati, mortis, et mundi."
12. Möhler, *Symbolik,* page 161-162.
13. *Ibid.,* page 162, "Si in fide fieri posset adulterium, peccatum non esset."

behind the cloak of justification, to issue a license for sin but rather to proclaim the wonders of unmerited grace. He does not say, "Sin till you are blue in the face," or "Sin for all you're worth," but "Sin bravely." With this word — whatever the libertine may do with it — he intends to exorcise the terrror of the believer who has discovered some sin in himself and has now lost sight of the grace of God. An abundance of grace can subdue the power of sin. Therefore Luther points on the one hand to the fact that we sin as long as we live and on the other to Christ who is the Conqueror of this world, of sin and death. In order to signalize the superabundance of grace, he contrasts it — Luther is a vehement man —with a thousand sinful enormities a day. His intention is not to yield quarter to Antinomianism but to upset a construction which would make sin and grace of equal weight, and therefore he exhorts the sinner to have courage. One would agree with Kattenbusch who says about these words of Luther: "It is rather a sentiment of the moment, and as such neither to be celebrated nor to be regretted but to be understood."

*   *   *

The Catholic polemic against the Reformation made one of its greatest mistakes, therefore, when it took the Reformed doctrine of forensic justification to mean no more than the "external" imputation of the righteousness of Christ, with no consequences for the inner man. From the confessional writings of the Reformation it may be shown, without danger of being at all obscure, that the real problems lie on a very different level from that on which Rome placed them.

The moment one is introduced to the Lutheran doctrine of sanctification he encounters the category of "the new obedience." The Confession of Augsburg did not, in reaction to the Roman work-righteousness, keep silent about the new obedience but treats of it in a separate article. It deals first with justification, and excludes all human merit; then comes a discussion of the office of the preacher through which, as a means used by the Holy Spirit, we receive faith; and further it confesses, in accord with the publications of Luther, that such faith must produce good fruit and good works and that the believer, although he cannot depend on such works for the favor of God, must perform them for God's sake. Here again we have an echo of the tremendous opposition there was to the meritoriousness of good works. This article concludes with a quotation from Ambrosius which contrasts the Sola-fide with the works of the law but which does not at all exclude the new obedience. On the contrary, it receives in the Sola-fide a sturdy foundation. This foundation, with its superstructure, becomes clearly visible in several other articles. In connection with the article on repentance there is a discussion of the fruits of repentance — a la John the Baptist — and of the moral improvement which should follow.

Especially important is the article[14] on the relation between faith and good works. There is here a strong protest against the charge of Antinomianism voiced by Catholics. "Our people are falsely accused of prohibiting good works." The reply to this incrimination is that works can never reconcile us with God: reconciliation is by faith and grace alone. To explain this reconciliation on the basis of good works would be to despise the Christ and to oppose the gospel. Not by works but by faith is the conscience set at ease. Only in the way of faith — but then indeed — does the Holy Spirit grant us good works "for God's sake and to his praise." And so the doctrine concerning faith should not be attacked but rather commended. In the absence of faith and trust in God, evil lusts hold sway in our hearts. Hence a true faith is the key to good works.

* * *

Later confessions concur with this great credo of the Lutheran churches. First to be mentioned is the Apology of

---

14. Article XX of the Augsburg Confession.

Melanchthon in which he defends the *Confessio Augustana* from attack. There was every reason for such an Apology, because the Augsburg creed had been rejected as untenable and inadequate by a "Confutatio Pontificia." In this confutation the Sola-fide was under strenuous attack, and numerous passages were adduced to "prove" the meritorious nature of good works, so that the confession should needs be thought inimical to what had been taught in the church since Saint Augustine.

Against these and similar reproaches Melanchthon writes his Apology. He treats in great detail of faith and works and the new obedience, giving prominence to its contrast with Antinomianism. There is not a trace in the Reformation, says he, of the supposed fixity of man's moral condition; as if faith were merely the reception of some obscure, external righteousness. It is quite otherwise. Once we have been justified through faith we must keep the law. He mentions the decalogue by name. The Holy Spirit creates a new life in the heart of the believer so that faith may revivify it. This renewal is the reception, in the heart, of God's law. Regenerated through faith we begin to fear God, to love and praise him, and to obey his will. Without faith and outside of Christ none of this is possible. Without the Holy Spirit the law cannot be fulfilled.

The Apology says of opponents of the Reformation that they know the second, but not the first, table of the decalogue; it is the first table — rather the first commandment, they need most of all. But whoever understands the meaning of faith and at the same time his own impotence — outside of Christ — will understand also that he must keep the law. Unjust, therefore, is the accusation that the Reformers do not teach good works. The contrary is true. But Melanchthon would have them come from the heart "lest they should be malicious, empty, cold, hypocritical works."

Van Duinkerken was impressed by the frequency with which Luther refers to the devil and concludes that the devil was too much for Luther and hence that Luther finds an escape by way of "faith alone." He may meet the devil also in Melanchthon's Apology and that in a very striking context. The Apology recognizes man's weakness in facing a devouring devil but adds, immediately, that the risen Christ is stronger than he. Since we through faith share in the conquest, we may, as promised, ask for protection against the evil one. Faith, in the end, is decisive. Good works witness to that faith. The power of the promise may not, by reliance on good works, be subverted. Extensively Melanchthon shows why it is faith, and not love, which justifies. His aim is throughout to keep good works pure and, as is true in all Lutheran symbols, all his arguments revolve around the Sola-fide. Good works are needful, and when they spring from faith, good indeed, but they can never provide any kind of ground for salvation. Good works are required not by coercion but from a glad and loving heart.

All this is proof abundant that the doctrines of Luther may not be viewed as antinomian. The "sola" in "sola-fide" is exclusive, to be sure, but this exclusiveness is there to point out the only possibility of good works. Already in the six-teenth century this principle was misunderstood. The "sola" was thought to be directed against good works. Bellarminus was one such writer who could not understand why "sola-fide" should exclude works but not faith since faith was after all a good work as well! The opposition to justification by love seemed to Catholic polemicists a devaluation of love, even though elsewhere in the Reformed confessions love did receive its due. The Reformation was not understood — evidence that people were caught hopelessly in work-righteousness and in the identification of faith and love. It is to the glory of the Lutheran creeds that they never capitulated on this point. Together with the Reformed symbols they have preserved the Gospel from the infiltration of supposedly meritorious good works, and they have honored and proclaimed the Gospel of grace.

*   *   *

On the more important points there is remarkable similarity between these statements and the Reformed confessions. In these, too, it is clear that faith is not merely an intellectual affirmation of a distant and alien righteousness but that it is a power which renews man and expresses itself in good works. We do find, in these creeds, repeated rejection of the works of the law, but this rejection does not in the least concern good works as signs and witnesses of faith. On the contrary: the bond between faith and works receives strong emphasis.

The Heidelberg Catechism declares, at the very outset, that our comfort in life and death is that we are saved through the blood of Jesus Christ and that by the Holy Spirit he assures us of eternal life and makes us heartily willing and ready, henceforth, to live unto him.[15] On the strength of our natural gifts and powers this cannot be accomplished. Our depravity is entire, unless we are regenerated by the Holy Spirit.[16] This regeneration is not a possibility but a reality which we know and confess by faith. An important section of the Catechism is devoted therefore to gratitude. Here full justice is done to the law and to the significance of the ten commandments for Christian living.

Not only the third section of the Catechism, however, inquires into this new obedience. In numerous Lord's Days the new life comes to the surface: in being governed by Word and Spirit,[17] in sharing the annointing of Christ and in the fulfilment of his three-fold office,[18] in being free from the evil lusts of the flesh through the sacrifice and death of Christ,[19] in being

---

15. *The Heidelberg Catechism,* Lord's Day 1.
16. Lord's Day 3.
17. Question 31.
18. Question 32.
19. Question 43.

raised to a new life through the resurrection of Christ,[20] in receiving the Spirit as an earnest,[21] in the communion of the saints and our duties to our fellow members,[22] and in the life-long battle against our sinful nature.[23]

There is special emphasis on the question whether the doctrine of justification does not make men careless and profane. The answer shows clearly the natural bond between faith and works. Justification by faith cannot leave the heart untouched, "for it is impossible that those who are implanted into Christ by a true faith should not bring forth the fruits of thankfulness."[24] Lord's Day 32 deals in particular with the necessity of good works and indicates their importance for our lives. With an appeal to Scripture the possibility of salvation conjoined with an ungodly life is rejected.

For a definition of good works we take Lord's Day 33 which also asserts their relation to true faith.[25] In its elucidation of the decalogue, the Catechism declares the law to be imperative for the believer and speaks of what God requires[26] and forbids,[27] of what the commandment teaches[28] and what we may not do.[29]

The Belgic Confession speaks in a similar vein, especially in the article on man's sanctification and good works.[30] It is said here that a true faith, which is worked in man by the operation of the Holy Spirit, "regenerates him and makes him a new man, causing him to live a new life and freeing him from the bondage of sin." Far from viewing the imputation of Christ's righteousness as external, ineffectual jugglery, it

---

20. Question 45.
21. Question 49.
22. Question 55.
23. Question 56.
24. Question 64.
25. Question 91.
26. Question 94, 103, 111.
27. Question 106, 107, 109, 110.
28. Question 108.
29. Question 97, 101, 102.
30. Article XXIV.

regards it as the open door to a life of good works. Justifying faith does not disincline men to good works, for without it they would act only out of self-love and fear of damnation. Faith is to be the foundation of good works. And it follows from the nature of faith which clings to divine grace that it cannot possibly be unfruitful. Appealing to Galatians 5:6, the article says that faith works through love and "excites man to the practice of those works which God has commanded in his Word."

There are in this article a number of expressions which are very important for the doctrine of good works. Good works, it says, must proceed from "the good root of faith." Only then are they good and acceptable in the sight of God, "forasmuch as they are all sanctified by his grace." Like the Lutheran symbols, it rejects the error that good works can be of any account towards our justification. However pleasing they are to God they have no justifying power. We are justified by faith in Christ, even before we do good works; otherwise they could not be good works, any more than the fruit of a tree can be good before the tree itself is good.

To the performance of good works, faith is not a deterrent but a stimulus. Only, having been instructed by the parable of the unprofitable servants, we would not ascribe merit to good works. Our works merit nothing.

Finally the article asserts that it does not deny that God rewards good works, but that it is through *his grace* that he crowns his gifts. The article concludes, we may say, with a confession of guilt: we do no work but what is polluted by our flesh and therefore we may not rely on anything but the suffering and death of our Savior. A side-glance at the article on justification through faith may give us further clarity: Jesus Christ imputes to us all his merits, as well as the "holy works which he has done for us and in our stead." Our righteousness is not that of the works of the law but that of faith, "an instrument that keeps us in communion with him in all his benefits which, when they become ours, are more than sufficient to acquit us of our sins."

Not only Article XXIV, therefore, but the entire confession presents to us the "new obedience of faith." Faith is not inactive, cannot be inactive, but operates in our common daily life. And that life of faith is evident from these marks: to wit, "by faith, and when, having received Jesus Christ the only Savior, they avoid sin, follow after righteousness, love the true God and their neighbor, neither turn aside to the right or left, and crucify the flesh with the works thereof."[31] With rare vigilance the confession guards against a perverted view of the Christian life. Concurrently with the confession of good works there is always a confession of great weakness against which the believer fights through the Spirit all the days of his life, continually taking refuge in the blood, death, passion, and obedience of our Lord Jesus Christ in whom he has remission of sins, through faith in him.

One may say that the confessions proceed always from faith to works and thence back to faith. This interconnection and order is a typical feature of Reformation doctrine: thus maintaining the bond between justification and sanctification, over against the "abstraction" of good works, it walked in the ways of Holy Scripture. The conclusion we may infer from all these data is that we can, according to Reformed belief, speak truly of sanctification *only* when we have understood the exceptionally great significance of the bond between Sola-fide and sanctification. We may never speak of sanctification as if we are entering — having gone through the gate of justification — upon a new, independent field of operation; sanctification does not come about by the interaction of dynamic impulses already present. We might, of course, speak of the "dunamis" of the Holy Spirit but this divine power comes to us only via our faith and may not be separated from it. That

31. Article XXIX (The marks of the true church, and wherein it differs from the false church).

is the unmistakable testimony of the Reformation.

And in teaching this the Reformation stood foursquare on Holy Scripture. Because the Sola-fide of the Reformation was not one-sided sectarianism or a weakening of the reality of salvation but a confession of "By grace alone are we saved" — *therefore* the Sola-fide is the only sound foundation for sanctification.

Wishing to correct the errors of false teachers in the church at Colosse, Paul points to the full salvation it has in Christ Jesus and reminds the church of the complete and radical nature of this salvation. "He delivered us out of the power of darkness, and translated us into the kingdom of the Son of his love; in whom we have our redemption, the forgiveness of our sins" (Col. 1:13-14). The false teachers had made the Gospel complicated by insisting on all sorts of requirements contrary to the simple Gospel of Paul. But Paul reassures them and shields them and would have them keep their simple joy and hope (Col. 1:23).

In faith they have received the grace of the Lord Jesus Christ. From being enemies doing works of evil (Col. 1:21), they have become reconciled to God by the death of Jesus Christ (Col. 1:22). Hence Paul comforts them — himself a prisoner — amid possible tribulations, with these strange words: "For ye died, and your life *is* hid with Christ in God" (Col. 3:3). Having died with him and having been buried with him (Col. 2:12) in baptism — sign of their adoption — they can now mind the things that are above, and know their lives are hid with Christ in God, safe, secure from dangers, even from demonic powers, because Christ is their life (Col. 3:4). This is the hiddenness of the church, and from this hiddenness flow all the admonitions which came to the church at Colosse. Because Christ is their life and they have been translated, they have to put away many things (Col. 3:8) and be new people. As God's elect, holy and beloved, they must put on a heart of compassion, kindness, lowliness, meekness

(Col. 3:12) and sing hymns and psalms with grace in their hearts unto God (Col. 3:16).

"And whatsoever ye do, in word or in deed, do all in the name of the Lord Jesus, giving thanks to God the Father through him" (Col. 3:17).

That is the significance of the Sola-fide for Paul. And that is how closely faith is related to sanctification. After speaking of this hiddenness of the church with Christ in God, he can talk about wives and husbands, parents and children, servants and masters (Col. 3:18 ff.). This is not a new subject for discussion: it is all contained in the fulness of salvation in Christ Jesus. They must be concerned with only one thing. "Ye serve the Lord Christ" (Col. 3:24).

It was about this "mystery of Christ" (Col. 4:3) the Reformers spoke when they discussed Sola-fide' and sanctification. They spoke to an age in which there was a great eclipse of the Gospel, a time of great unrest. They spoke sharply and — it is no wonder — sometimes faultily. But they did give the essence of the Gospel message back to the people. This is clear from their own words but also from the words of the opposition. The Council of Trent minced no words in its repudiation of Sola-fide. For *this* Sola-fide and *this* ground for sanctity could not be tolerated by those who loved the Roman doctrine of grace and penance and meritorious good works. This was the dilemma, this the conflict!

Militia Christiana

CHAPTER III

Militia Christiana

ONCE the significance of Sola-fide has been established and the range of its relevancy explored — especially in regard to the forgiveness of sins — one's attention is bound to turn to the nature of the life that issues from justification. Though it be true that the doctrine of justification and the exhortation to holiness are compatible, there seems somehow to be a contradiction between the teaching of justification and sanctification on the one hand, and the awful truth about the lives actually lived by believers on the other.

Let the reader recall the earnestness with which Paul addresses the Corinthians as "they that are sanctified in Christ Jesus" and the concurrent passion with which he exposes their sins. Or bring to mind that, after pronouncing his benediction upon the Galatians, Paul declares them to be senseless, to be under the spell of evil men and hence disobedient to the truth (Gal. 3:1). What is the awful truth we are here confronting? What is the place of sin and lustfulness, not in the tumultuous breast of Luther this time, but in the Church of Paul's day to which he said that Christ gave himself for their sins? Indeed, there seems to be every reason to be puzzled at the Pauline question: "Who shall lay anything to the charge of God's elect?" (Rom. 8:33).

We seem still to be at sea as to whether the imputation of righteousness is merely external and without practical value; as to whether the abundance of grace (Rom. 5:17) is subject to severe limitations; and as to whether faith is working through love (Gal. 5:6) or whether it is practically impotent.

These are things hard to be understood, especially in the light of what Paul says: "We who died to sin, how shall we any longer live therein?" (Rom. 6:2). Or in the light of what Jesus says: "If therefore the son shall make you free, ye shall be free indeed" (John 8:36).

Where is this freedom, this sensational release from the past, this "erstwhile" of sin, and where is the proof of transfer into the kingdom? This being a new creature in Christ (Gal. 6:5), this standing fast in the Lord (Phil. 4:1), this grace that is "with us" — where and how do these things become apparent, visible? Then there is the mysterious identification with Christ, this being baptized in his death, this burial with him, this being united with him and having our old man crucified with him (Rom. 6:3-6) — what difference does it make in our everyday living?

Could it be — one hesitates to ask the question — that we are taking grace too seriously, that in considerable measure it is dependent on our own voluntary reactions? Let us turn our attention to the problem of the Sin of Believers.

*   *   *

It is no wonder that throughout the history of the Church and of theology the problem of sanctification came up with reference to these questions. At bottom it is the "Militia Christi" which causes all the perplexity: for why should continued warfare be necessary after the achievement of victory? after being crucified, dead, buried, and raised with Christ?

One answer known to Church history is the answer of Perfectionism. The phenomenon of Perfectionism is noteworthy because this doctrine seems quite at variance with observable facts — our continued sins and sinful nature — and interprets the inability to stumble (II Peter 1:10) as the inability to sin. Perfectionism presents a problem we may never lightly dismiss: the problem of the sin of those who *are* justified and whose sanctification is Christ himself. A faulty reaction to Perfectionism would be to assert that the imperfection of human life is a matter of course. One cannot fob off Perfectionism by saying "In many things we all stumble" (James 3:2) or "Wretched man that I am! who shall deliver me . . . ?" (Romans 7:24), for these utterances are not excuses for sin but confessions of sin.

There is in Perfectionism something which disturbs us and which, though it be generally of a sectarian nature, we must honestly confront. Some points at least are more important than that of apparent pride and an exaggerated estimate of self, an example of which, mentioned by Kuyper,[1] is that of the preacher who claimed from his pulpit that for an entire year he had managed to abstain from sin. This false estimate of self may be regrettable but we must not forget that it arose from a consideration, be it confused, of Scriptural teachings.

The crucial doctrine of Perfectionism is that it is possible for the believer, even before his death, to attain perfection. And the advocates of this doctrine think it proper to appeal to the numerous passages in the Bible which demand such perfection. It is to be expected, therefore, that Perfectionism will be of a decidedly activistic stamp. Bavinck points out that Perfectionism is common to nearly all nomists,[2] though we may not, of course, assume that it is merely a form of nomism. For one of the basic thoughts of this movement is that sanctification and justification are acts of God and *therefore* perfect.

Perfectionism does not first of all insist on a fatiguing and precarious walking of some ethical tightrope, the reward of which would be perfect holiness; its insistence is on holiness as a gift of God which includes not only release from guilt but also release from the power of sin.

To be sanctified is to be created anew, and this occurrence implies total alteration of human life. Antecedent to this re-

1. Abraham Kuyper, *E Voto*, Lord's Day 44.
2. Herman Bavinck, *Gereformeerde Dogmatiek*, IV, page 246ff.

newal is the justifying act of God — an act fully recognized by
Wesley, for instance, as proceeding from God alone. In this
respect he wished to agree with the Reformation. "Wesley
himself considered, that (*sic,* Tr.) in this doctrine he was in
full harmony with the attitude of the Reformation and many
modern scholars have agreed with him."[3] Perfectionism is
not attained by accumulating merit, according to him, but it
is a gift of God.

There is nothing in Wesley of a justification that is founded
on salvation as actually realized in man. Justification is justification of the ungodly and can only be appropriated in faith.
By good works no man is justified. All confidence must be
withdrawn from man and placed in reconciliation through
Christ. "In this attitude to justification Wesley is obviously
following Reformed principles."[4] Concurrent with this justification, however, is sanctification viewed as act of God. Indeed, the purpose of justification is not merely to impute righteousness but to realize it in man.

Leaving aside various nuances within Perfectionism, nuances ranging from the idea of the necessity of process in sanctification to the idea of its immediate and complete realization,
we would consider the unqualified appropriation of holiness
in the concrete, Perfectionistic sense of freedom from sin
through a faultless love. The assumption is that an acceptance through faith of the redemptive work of Christ gives to
the believer a part in it amid the commonplace reality of everyday life. Lindström has reproduced a conversation between
Wesley and Zinzendorf in which Wesley's view of sanctification becomes clearly apparent.[5]

Zinzendorf: I acknowledge no inherent Perfection. Christ is
only Perfection.

3. Harold Lindström, *Wesley and Sanctification.* Upsala, 1946, page 87.
4. *Ibid.,* page 90.
5. His view, namely, as it was in 1741.

Wesley: I believe the Spirit of Christ works Christian Perfection in true Christians.

Zinzendorf: By no means.   All our Perfection is in Christ. Faith in the Blood of Christ is the only Christian Perfection.   The whole Christian Perfection is imputed, not inherent.   We are perfect in Christ. We are never perfect in ourselves.

Wesley: Is not then every true Believer Holy?

Zinzendorf: Certainly.   But he is Holy in Christ, not in himself.

Wesley: But are not his Heart and Life Holy?

Zinzendorf: Undoubtedly.

Wesley: Is he not, by consequence, Holy in Himself?

Zinzendorf: No, no, only in Christ.   He is not Holy in Himself.   He has no Holiness at all in Himself.[6]

It is apparent from this conversation that Wesley wants to see sanctification in concrete forms. He says as it were: Faith alone is not enough. Of course, behind this concrete sanctification lies the justification which is its foundation, but he who is justified is nonetheless truly *made* holy. Hence Wesley does not glory in the works of the law but in the power of God working through the Holy Spirit. And this holiness may be "entire sanctification," though at times Wesley doubted whether it was attainable before death. The completeness of Christ's work can be maintained only, says Wesley, if it be reflected in human life. That work demands perfect love. Based on a profusion of Divine grace, this life cannot but be full of holiness and a reflection of the scintillating beauty of Christ's sacrificial suffering unto death.

In spite of his view of justification, however, Wesley had decided leanings toward Arminianism. He appears to have a

6. Lindström. *op. cit.*, page 137.

quarrel with the Reformation after all. He did not indeed make sanctification the ground for final justification — and any such criticism he opposed with great emphasis — but he was troubled by the problem of the necessity of good works and the distinction between merit and condition. In this connection he offered sharp opposition to the Reformed doctrines of election and irresistible grace and the perseverance of the saints.

Attention has been drawn to the synergistic element in Wesley's theology. This is the more striking because Wesley admitted full acceptance of the Sola-fide doctrine. Evidently one may accept the doctrine and then fail to do justice to it. For again and again there comes to the surface in his Perfectionism a strong nomistic tendency. Wesley did not fail to warn against a facile over-estimate of self, but an insidious nomism he did not entirely escape. As Lerch says; "Not only our reflection but also the subsequent course of the Holiness movement shows that there is here the threat either of legal rigorism or of overestimating the strength of one's own footing."[7]

Since Wesley proceeded emphatically from the justification of the ungodly, his synergism is a serious warning. The Sola-fide doctrine is subject to frequent misunderstanding. One can assume it as one's starting-point, as did Wesley, and subsequently view the process of sanctification in terms of a dynamic category — a power plus its effects — without taking account of the bearings which faith always sustains toward divine grace. Sola-fide becomes a point of departure and breaks its connections with sanctification. Here lies the cause of Wesley's tendency toward synergism, in spite of his adherence to Sola-fide. This tendency is not a count against Sola-fide

---

7. David Lerch, *Heil und Heiligung bei John Wesley*, 1941, page 137.

but a warning against misconceiving its all-important significance.

*   *   *

It will not do, however, to write off Perfectionism simply
because it has illicit relations with nomism and synergism.
The problem which Perfectionism throws into our laps is and
remains important.   It must be answered by an appeal to
Scripture.

Let us first of all consult our Confession.   Lord's Day 44,
for instance, is openly hostile to the central thesis of Perfectionism. "But can those who are converted to God keep these
commandments perfectly?" -- that is the question, and we
know what Perfectionism replies to it.   But this is the answer
of the Catechism: "No; but even the holiest men, while in this
life, have only a small beginning of this obedience; yet so that
with earnest purpose they begin to live, not only according to
some but according to all the commandments of God." In a later
chapter we shall return to this answer; at this point it is
enough to show that where Perfectionism says Yes, our Confession says No.

We shall have to unveil the portrait offered us by Scripture
of the church in general and of the believers individually.
And we shall find that while the Bible ascribes holiness to the
church, as well as other magnificent things, it continues to
view believers as sinners whose transgressions must be exposed and whose litanies of guilt are recorded.[8]   Perfectionism
does not deny all this but teaches, at the same time, that the
believer is able completely to transcend the pollution of sin.
In this respect there is considerable agreement between Perfectionism and Catholicism.

Rome teaches not only the possibility of moral perfection
but also the presence of perfection through the infusion of
sanctifying grace in baptism.   Although this perfection may

---

8. Compare Herman Bavinck, *Gereformeerde Dogmatiek*, IV, pages 246,
247.

easily be lost, through the power of grace it is once actual. According to Rome one takes part in the supernatural life of God through baptism; and so it brands the Reformed view of sin as pessimistic. Concupiscence may still be present in the baptized person, but it is certainly no longer of a sinful character. In justification human sin, according to Rome, is not merely covered but actually eradicated.[9]

Rome does not deny that human life must be a warfaring life, for the battle may, upon the loss of sanctification, have to be resumed. The only remaining choice is the way of penance until the end. The perspective of Perfectionism conflicts with this view, since it does not, as Catholic doctrine, identify justification with sanctification, and provides for a life evolving from justification into attainable perfection. The question we are entertaining is whether there is warrant in Scripture for this optimism.

Did the Reformers perhaps expect too little of the justified believer? Did they, on account of their "pessimistic" view of original sin, detract from the power of grace? Or is their confessional legacy, Lord's Day 44, for instance, a true replica of the Scriptural portrait of the believer?

This enquiry concerns not merely Wesleyan Methodism but a number of modern trends as well. Especially Paul Althaus has tried to show that the Reformation, as tested by Scripture, has gone off at a tangent. The quarrel would be with the apostle Paul who was convinced, according to Althaus, of the believer's perfectibility on earth. Luther and Calvin were wrong, then, in teaching that the believer does not attain moral perfection and stands throughout his life in need of the forgiveness of sins. Says Althaus: "According to Paul, the Christian who is perfect has made a clean break with sin," and "the renewing power of Christ secures blamelessness (Untadeligkeit) for the Christian in his life upon earth."[10] Not sinful-

---

9. Bartmann, *Dogmatik*, II, pages 76, 103
10. Paul Althaus, *Paulus und Luther über den Menschen*, 1938, page 70.

ness was the dominant problem, on Paul's view, but mortality. Windisch also asserts that Paul was exempt from a continual sense of sin and delighted himself rather in Christ. Believers are saints in the full sense of the word. "A saint is a man in whom the power of sin has been broken, whose manner of life before God and men is spotless, who in his life and in his spiritual stature exemplifies holiness and integrity."[11]

This representation of the believer has little in common with that of the Reformed confessions. Besides Lord's Day 44, there is the interpretation of the fifth petition of the Lord's prayer as given in Lord's Day 51. Believers are said to turn to God to pray: "Be pleased, for the sake of Christ's blood, not to impute to us, miserable sinners, any of our trangressions, nor *the evil which always cleaves to us.*"[12] And in Lord's Day 21 the believer admits his sinful nature against which, he says, he must struggle all his life long.[13]

Hence the warfare of the Christian is indissolubly connected with his sinful nature; and we are bound to consider whether the confessions have indeed left us a pessimistic anthropology; and whether modern Pietism is right in telling us: "Luther and other Reformers were men of little faith. They have not sufficiently relied on Jesus Christ. They have not experienced his sanctifying power as Paul."[14]

Pivotal in the discussion of the believer's status is undoubtedly the seventh chapter of the epistle to the Romans. This chapter has been the occasion of frequent discussion in the history of theology. It was feared that the Reformation had imposed its own arbitrary interpretation upon it. The issue more precisely was: Who is the subject speaking in the verses 14 to 25?

Augustine judged, first, that the speaker was man in general and later that it was the struggling Christian. This new exe-

11. H. Windish, *Paulus und Christus,* 1934, page 258.
12. *The Heidelberg Catechism,* Question 126.
13. Question 56.
14. Paul Althaus, *op. cit.,* page 72.

gesis enabled him the better to fight Pelagianism since it provided him with proof for original sin. In his Commentary on Romans, Calvin takes note of Augustine's shift and attributes it, not to exegetical tyranny, but to increasing subjection to the Scriptures.[15] Althaus deplores all this, speaks of dogmatic prejudice, and arrives by what he calls historical exegesis at the view that Chapter 7 does not speak of the Christian conflict, and cannot because the Christian believer is not given the floor until Chapter 8. Only the believer's heart is the arena of flesh and Spirit. But Romans 7 nowhere mentions the Spirit. It relates the fierce contest waged in the human Ego between flesh and mind. From this contest there is no escape: Who shall deliver me out of the body of this death?

To say that the "I" of Romans 7 is Paul or the Christian in general — continues Althaus — is to deny the power of the Spirit which opposes *and subdues* the murky powers of the flesh. Does not Paul say that believers are freed from the dominion of the flesh? And is it not natural to conclude that the speaker of Romans 7 cannot be the believer but must be man "under the law"? Althaus adds that it is man "under the law" as the believer sees him. Only as X-rayed by the Gospel is the natural man truly visible in his pathetic state. Nonetheless this Christian diagnosis is not unrelated to the natural man's own view of himself. The picture Paul paints here is a heightened reproduction of this man's self-portrait.

Paul is depicting a conflict, a Widerspruch, in the unconverted man. This conflict is not a conflict, as in the believer, between flesh and Spirit, but nonetheless a very real, a very fatiguing, conflict. The flesh is not allowed to run riot; it has an opponent, namely, mind, conscience, the inner man. The natural man, endorsing the Law, does what he would not, even what he hates. Man without Christ even says that not he, but the sin that made its home in him, is responsible for the evil

15. Calvin's Commentary on Chapter 7.

that he does, and he insists that at heart he delights in the Law of God. There is a schism in his soul and the antagonists are equiponderant.

Althaus now faces the necessity of fitting this picture into the total scheme of Paul's views. And so he refers back to what Paul says in Romans 1 and 2, about the heathen. Man without Christ has a delight in the Law. This attitude is possible only if the Spirit is already at work within him. Hence in Romans 1 and 2 Paul must presuppose a general operation of the Holy Spirit.

The Reformation brusquely characterized the unconverted man as "flesh" while Paul sees him — natural man — racked by conflict. This fact the Reformation simply ignored. It pictured man without Christ in grim revolt against divine grace, not as Paul, who saw in the prior conflict a point of contact with this man. Not that there is a gradual incline from unconverted to converted man; but the Holy Spirit does not simply veto every element in that natural man, at least not insofar as he is amenable to the will of God. It is a mistake to speak brutally, as did Luther, of the hatred of the natural man against the Law of God. Whoever does full justice to the Scriptures will find that the idealistic man is not entirely indocile in face of the Gospel. For that Gospel makes manifest the agonizing schism of the heart and brings relief.

It is to be expected that the exegesis of humanists will run in the same rut. Erasmus, for instance, also rejects the idea that Paul is speaking of himself in Chapter 7. Basic to humanistic exegesis is the division of man into higher and lower capacities, the lower being the source of evil. This contrast between high and low, good and evil, was awarded metaphysical status in the definition of man and makes of no effect Paul's warning: "Let us cleanse ourselves from all defilement of flesh and spirit. . ." (II Cor. 7:1).

We need not at all deny that the Reformers were influenced, in their exegesis of this passage, by their understanding of the total Scriptural analysis of man. This is evident in Calvin's assertion that the conflict here depicted by Paul is found only in the recipient of the Holy Spirit. The man who is left to his own natural devices is a stranger to this conflict. Calvin protests against the philosophers who describe the human mind in terms of this conflict and contraposes with this view the Scriptural doctrine of the evil heart. He recalls the sophists who appealed to Romans 7 to fortify their conception of free will. In the natural man, says Calvin, there is never any hatred of sin. Althaus may still be murmuring about dogmatic prejudice, but Calvin cannot help recognizing the natural impression received from this chapter — from the dominant first person singular — and does not wish to arrive by way of distinctions between high and low at an anthropology that cannot stand the test of Scripture. Since the natural interpretation of Romans 7 coincides with the over-all testimony of Scripture, there is no reason to abandon it.

Paul saw the natural man as an object of God's wrath (Rom. 1), and speaks of children of wrath (Eph. 2:3), led by the spirit that works in the sons of disobedience (Eph. 2:2), dead through sin and trespasses (Eph. 2:5), full of the works of the flesh (Gal. 5:19). Of the mind of the flesh Paul says that is death and enmity against God; "for it is not subject to the law of God, neither indeed can it be" (Rom. 8:5-7). It was further reflection on these truths which led Augustine to alter his views on Romans 7.

*   *   *

Suppose we assume at this point that what Paul has sketched for us in Romans 7 is the profile of the battling believer. We have then an excellent basis for further reflection on the Perfectionistic view of man. Then this chapter affords us, in plaintive tones, a confession *de profundis,* a confession born of the meekness of the Spirit-touched heart. It has often been said that this picture of the believer clashes head-on with that of Romans 8, where Paul says that the law of the Spirit of life made us free from the law of sin and of death (Rom. 8:2) ; and with Romans 6, where we read: "For sin shall not have dominion over you" (Rom. 6:14). Do we not have here an expression of a more optimistic view than is expected from reading that doleful Chapter 7? Let us select for consideration some of its more striking laments:

1. ". . .I am carnal, sold under sin" (verse 14).

2. ". . .For not what I would, that do I practice; but what I hate that I do" (verse 15).

3. "For I know that in me, that is, in my flesh, dwelleth no good thing; for to will is present with me, but to do that which is good is not" (verse 18).

4. "Wretched man that I am! who shall deliver me out of the body of this death?" (verse 24).

In these verses Paul depicts sin as an all-pervasive power. As a result sin has ruled as lord. That power still affects the believer. This is evident in the expression: sold under sin. We have heard these words before, namely in the indictment which Elijah pronounced against Ahab: "I have found thee, because thou hast sold thyself to do that which is evil in the sight of Jehovah" (I Kings 21:20, 25).

Need we infer from this that Ahab's life and Paul's are describable in the same terms? Does this perhaps illustrate the justification of the wicked and the supposed fact that justification is a merely objective relation inoperative in the heart, this "sold under sin"? A comparison between Paul and Ahab, however, shows at least one important difference: Paul says he *has been* sold under sin, whereas Elijah throws into Ahab's teeth that he has sold himself. In the case of Ahab we have simon-pure hostility to God and an unconditional surrender to the Evil One. In the case of Paul we have sin as an overpowering force which makes him cry out against it — granted that he is not exempt from responsibility for it. But to say as Paul does that he finds himself doing what he really loathes is impossible for Ahab.   Ahab does the evil he relishes and rejects the clear commandment of God.   He pursues his career in single-minded dedication to evil.   Even in his being sold under sin, in the daily experience of being overpowered, Paul is not a slave to sin.   Servants of sin –– that is what believers used to be; now they are servants of righteousness (Rom. 6:17-18).

Whoever thinks he has been treated to an intolerable contradiction is probably the victim of the effort to make this duality psychologically transparent.   He is a dupe indeed: there is no transparency here, only grief over sin, meekness, confession of guilt, and a glorying in salvation (Rom. 7:25).

We are here privy both to Paul's confession of being sold under sin and led captive (Rom. 7:23) and to his sudden upsurge of joy over belonging, after all, to his Lord, Jesus Christ. This picture of the schismatic heart is surely different from that of the unbroken spirit of the natural man (Rom. 3:10-18).   Paul creates by his self-complaint a curious dissociation. The evidence here of a fractured heart has even been called the doctrine of the dual Ego; for in verse 18 Paul says in him, that is, in his flesh, sin has made its home, while in verse 20 he says it is not he, but sin, that does evil.   And the question has arisen whether Paul's complaints do not evince a very defective psychology.   Paul may say, "it is not I," but what right has he to dissociate himself from his own sins?   How can he speak of being sold and not mean that he wilfully sells himself every day?   And how can he in spite of all this still speak of his Lord?   Does not his sin proceed from his heart whence are the most deep-rooted issues of life?   Is not this dissociation from sin a flight from responsibility?   And of what use is all this ambiguous talk?

These questions arise naturally and, as long as we do not drag in any pedantic preconception as to Paul's knowledge of psychology, there is hope we shall find an answer.

Paul continually refers to the arch-contention which arose in his soul upon his encounter with Jesus Christ. He refers to it not in order to excuse his repeated lapsing into sin but to express the irruption of grace into his life, an irruption which abolished his self-exaltation and pride. Upon the fragments of his ruined self now rises the drama of perpetual conflict. And this psychic discordancy is a thing for which he thanks God and a sign, strangely enough, of a finally achieved peace. The conflict does not break his soul in two, each part flying at the throat of the other, but signifies the entering in of the Holy Spirit. Every attempt to make this heterogeneity transparent to the eye by some division of human functions is doomed to failure.

When Kuyper distinguishes between the central and the peripheral part of the soul and declares the centre already "glorified,"[16] we must demur, however laudable his effort in explaining Romans 7; for this division of man into center and periphery, flesh and spirit, is a denial of the fact that we are here concerned with the Spirit's operation in the whole of man.

Paul knows that the believer is constantly embroiled in a conflict which issues into growing alienation. Human existence lies beneath the benediction and in the clutch of grace. Rather than analyze the resultant duality in anthropological terms, Paul adduces two related events: a cry of contrition over sins committed and a cry of victory through a conquering Christ, the events corresponding to his being a captive to sin and a bondservant to Christ. This conflict is not a poignant tragedy played behind closed curtains; at the decisive moment it breaks through the chrysalis of a windowless past and breathes hope and humility.

In his exegesis of Romans 7, Karl Barth once asked: "Who will guarantee me that the "I" who does what he pleases and the other "I" who deplores what the former does are not at

---

16. Abraham Kuyper, *Gemeene Gratie*, II, page 323.

bottom identical? Or that all my grim decisions against myself are not in the end a futile comedy ("Münchausiade," Tr.) which is played within the four walls of the house of sin that is I?"[17] Apparently Barth wishes to warn against a false contentment over the presence of conflict. It is possible within the boundaries of our souls, Barth warns, to stray into the hinterland of Pietistic logic. In confronting Paul's act of self-dissociation Barth fears that a perfunctory exegesis could easily splinter the totality of human corruption. He opposes any division of man into a sinful and a sinless section. From this premise, itself correct, he proceeds to the conclusion that it is nonsense to speak of an "I" that is beyond the sin that dwells in him, since mention is made of only one reality, the reality of sin. Along this route he arrives at the following result: "Reality, also the reality of religion, knows but one man and that man is I — no other. And this One, willing and not achieving, not willing and succeeding, lives within the four walls of the house of sin."[18]

It appears that Barth fails to do justice to the dissociation Paul has indicated and to the conflict he has signalized. What Paul does he knows not and he looks upon it with aversion (Rom. 7:15). He wills the good, and evil he wills not (Rom. 7:19). He delights in the law of God "after the inward man" (Rom. 7:22). Though Paul's endorsement of the law of God is positive, there is not a speck of self-satisfaction in it. The flesh takes him captive even while he is attracted to the law of God. Through the window of his faith he views the victory that is on its way to the battle-field. And as his gratitude grows, so does his grief over remaining sins.

It is striking that Paul, having mentioned his delight in the law of God, proceeds immediately to that other law, the law he sees in his members. Here again Paul does not describe a section of himself that is still subject to sin, as distin-

17. Karl Barth, *Römerbrief*, page 245.
18. *Ibid.*, page 248.

quished from another section that is not, but he etches his entire self as under the direction of his evil heart it still contends against the invincible grace of his Lord.

Wretched man that I am!

The subject of Romans 7 is not the natural man as seen by the believer, but the believing child of God as by the grace of God he has learned to see himself. From this knowledge is born his confession of guilt. From this knowledge, too, springs his daily tussle with himself. It is surely not a tussle without tension. Woe to him who would rest upon grace as upon *his* laurels and forget the law of sin in his members! Whatever hope there is must be of faith.

* * *

In any discussion of Militia Christiana — the warfare which key-notes the Christian life — both the "militia" and the "Christiana" need to be emphasized. Neither may be neglected. The "Christiana" may not weaken but must motivate the warfare. In addition, there is the danger that, when the victory of Christ is lost sight of, the warfare degenerates into self-reliant activism.

The true Militia Christiana can be waged only from the incentives of Romans 7: humility and gratitude. This warfare is taught throughout the New Testament; and everywhere we hear the confession of guilt: "If we say we have no sin, we deceive ourselves, and the truth is not in us" (I John 1:8, 10). This confession is the ground in the New Testament for every warning, admonition, and indictment directed at the Christian Church.

When Perfectionism began to teach a "second blessing" it was on the road to making sanctification independent from justification. Justification was cited to prove the possibility of this "second blessing." And so people began to distinguish those who had the "second blessing" from those who

were less advanced. This distinction amounts to a denial of
the unity of the Church and of the reality of sin which, according to the Scriptures, still dwells in the believer. Perfectionism could not therefore escape the bane of activism and nomism. The perfection of which it spoke was a rational infer-
ence from the doctrine of justification and hence the possibility of moral perfection and of a "second" blessing bore a
speculative character.

The Scriptures always speak of sanctification in the existential sphere of faith. Paul speaks of "perfecting holiness in
the fear of God" (II Cor. 7:1). Holiness is never a "second
blessing" placed next to the blessing of justification; it has an
inviolable place of its own in the scheme of Apostolic teaching.
The Scriptures do mention perfection: "Ye therefore shall be
perfect, as your heavenly Father is perfect" (Matt. 5:48).
And to the rich young ruler comes the advice: "If thou would-
est be perfect, go, sell that which thou hast, and give to the
poor. . ." (Matt. 19:21). But in the Bible perfection is never
presented apart from faith. Our completion is only realized
in Christ (Col. 2:10) "for by one offering he hath perfected
for ever them that are sanctified" (Heb.10:14). The exhortation which comes to the Church is that it must live in faith
out of this fullness; not that it must work for a second blessing, but that it must feed on the first blessing, the forgiveness
of sins. The warfare of the Church, according to Scriptural
testimony, springs from the demand really to live from this
first blessing.

God has chosen us that we should be holy and blameless
before him. To that end Christ sacrificed himself. His purpose was that "he might present the church to himself a glorious church, not having spot or wrinkle. . ." (Eph. 5:27).
There are many times when this "holy and blameless" has a
definite eschatological accent; that is, this admonition touches
all of human life until, and in the interest of, the return of
Christ. Hearts are established in order that they may be "un-

blamable in holiness before our God and Father, at the coming of our Lord Jesus with all his saints" (I Thess. 3:13). This admonition does not imply that we can slacken our vigilance today and tomorrow, but only that the Church is under the pressure of Christ's return.

In view of this orientation toward the re-advent of Christ, it is reasonable that the Scriptures should nowhere speak of antecedent periods of perfection. Nowhere does the Bible teach the possibility of attaining perfection before the great consummation. All of life is to be viewed eschatologically and all the saints must perfect their holiness in the fear of God. Neither the perfecting, nor the fear of God, may be neglected. To strike out on the way to perfection on our own power and to cut the cords with which we are tied to Christ is to make impossible that we shall "be preserved entire, without blame at the coming of our Lord Jesus Christ" (I Thess. 5:23).

We might still ask whether there is any explanation for the fluctuating course of the life of believers — the many things in which we stumble, as James says. Could it be explained perhaps from the way in which God is known to act in our lives? Is our prayer that God will not regard our sinful nature required perhaps by the manner in which the Holy Spirit chooses to operate? Many have talked in this fashion and pointed to the variation discernible in God's dealings with man. They refer to the variability of conversions: how God brings to the life of one man utter and instantaneous collapse and rehabilitation and to the life of another a change as gradual as the growth of an embryo and as unwavering as a sunrise.

Is it possible to attribute our residual sinfulness to a retarding and restraining action of the Holy Spirit?

We are obviously walking on dangerous ground. For we may never establish a causal connection between a "partial" working of the Holy Spirit and our imperfection. We consider ourselves advised on his point by the reticence of Scripture. And if a reckless logicism should lead anyone to such a conclusion we may well ask how he could square it with the repeated admonitions and promises which must regulate us. The way of dogmatic logicism is not that of faith, which always listens, listens, . . . to the Word. The end of such sophism would be the hideous heresy: God is responsible for sin, also for remaining sin.

The reaction of faith will be to shrink back from this thought and to press on toward the goal — the reward of being called by God in Christ (Phil. 3:14). And the believer will speak in the language of Militia Christiana: "Not that I have already obtained, or am already made perfect: but I press on, if so be that I may lay hold on that for which also I was laid hold on by Christ Jesus" (Phil. 3:12).

Throughout God's Word we run into the idiom of struggle. And confession of guilt is especially common with those who know the fellowship of God. The call of the believer is always a psalm *de profundis*. It is man in touch with grace who cries: "If thou, Jehovah, shouldest mark iniquities, O Lord, who could stand?" (Ps. 130:3). Not the child of wrath but the servant of God says: "And enter not into judgment with thy servant; for in thy sight no man living is righteous" (Ps. 143:2).

It is before the throne of grace that guilt reveals itself. Self-complaint is a natural product of communion with God. When John speaks of walking in the light in which God dwells, he immediately begins to witness to the blood that cleanses us (I John 1:7). It is when we confront the glory and grace of God that we realize we still stumble in many ways (James 3:2).

To speak of the Church is to speak of the struggle to remain children of God in communion with him and to live gratefully in virtue of the forgiveness of sin. This life of sanctification proceeds in weakness, temptation, and exposure to the powers of darkness. Hence the life of the believer is fenced in with admonitions: "Ye have not yet resisted unto blood, striving against sin" (Heb. 12:4). Or in the incisive words of Paul: "Neither give place to the devil" (Eph. 4:27), or of James: "Resist the devil" (James 4:7).

All these admonitions are expressions of divine grace. Grace prompted Paul to rage against the sins of the Corinthian Church, against such fornication as is not even among the Gentiles (I Cor. 5:1), against pride (I Cor. 5:2), against greed and irreverence (I Cor. 11:21).

Perfectionism is a premature seizure of the glory that will be: an anticipation leading irrevocably to nomism. The "second blessing" constitutes the link.

The believer, who understands his justification and views his life against the backdrop of Divine grace, will gain a deeper knowledge of his own sinfulness. When Peter, stupefied by the wonderful catch of fish, confronts the goodness of his Master, he cries out: "Depart from me; for I am a sinful man, O Lord!" (Luke 5:8). Surrounded by the radiance of the Master, Peter can only bow his head. Later those other words were to cut through the night: "If all shall be offended in thee, I will never be offended" (Matt. 26:33). By these words Peter meant to envelop Christ with his fidelity and love. Christ must here bathe in Peter's glory, not Peter in Christ's. We know the outcome.

Not these words, but rather those spoken over the bonanza of fish, belong to the Militia Christiana.

The Genesis of Sanctification

CHAPTER IV

The Genesis of Sanctification

IN THIS and the succeeding chapter we shall discuss separately the beginning and the progress of sanctification. Though the two belong together it will prove valuable thus to organize several points of discussion.

Whereas in regard to the progress of sanctification there is always anxiety lest this process be understood as biological evolution, in regard to the beginning of sanctification we face the problem of the change or renewal of human life. There has been and will always be considerable debate as to whether sanctification actually effects a change in the believer, or whether divine forgiveness merely enables him to view his old, unaltered life from a fresh angle. We are here vis-a-vis the problem often expressed in the words: *Simul justus et peccator*, that is, being righteous and at the same time a sinner. Even today the debate concerning sanctification often centers around these words. The charge is that people have lost sight of the serious implications of the "simul" so that now it is past dallying time for us to highlight its critical and paradoxical meaning.

At first blush it seems incredible that this expression should evoke a difference of opinion. Apart from a handful of Perfectionists almost anybody is willing to recognize the presence of this dual aspect; and no one would want to erase either the "justus" or the "peccator." There is a general consensus that the justified sinner remains, to his dying day, a sinner.

Further analysis discloses, however, that the discussion arises from the ascription of various meanings to these words.

Are the "justus" and the "peccator" of equal weight? Are they two foci of equal doctrinal interest, or is the one of primary, the other of secondary importance?

These questions touch especially Luther, who had a particular fondness for them. And in his same area we encounter the words of St. Augustine: "In part justified, in part sinner."[1] In this formula lie many problems we must analyze in order to gain an understanding of sanctification.

In Luther's commentary on the epistle to the Romans especially, this two-fold truth creeps to the surface. He presents it in numerous ways. The believer, says Luther, is like a sufferer of some disease who has been told by his physician that he will surely be cured. Hence the believer is both ill and well — but only well in the prediction of the doctor. Catholic writers have cited this example as being typically in accord with the Reformed doctrine of justification. The cure of sin, they aver, is implicit in the word of promise but never becomes real. The ill person expects complete recovery, not because he feels restoring forces at work in his body, but because he relies on a promise. So the significance of "being righteous and at the same time a sinner" would be: righteous by divine imputation, a sinner in reality. The justified man would not himself fulfil the law. His righteousness is merely the cloak that covers; his sinfulness the nasty truth that remains.

There can be little doubt that this description is not faithful to Luther's view. He does indeed see the sinner as justified by divine verdict but he likewise sees this justified sinner in a state of convalescence. Believers are involved in a process of recovery and hence Luther can speak of being "in part justified, in part sinner." The inclination toward evil remains but there is a transition nonetheless toward righteousness. To pray for the total suspension of sin, says Luther, is to ask for the suspension of life. The children of God could never com-

---

1. "Ex quadam parte justus, ex quadam parte peccator."

pletely subdue the Jebusites. And the parable of the Good Samaritan shows, says he, that the victim of the robbers needed not only to have his wounds bound up but also to have the inn-keeper take care of him.

This fact of partial recovery Luther has broached in many similes: the first-fruits of the total harvest, the restoration of a ruined house, the cloth which in the hands of a tailor becomes an article fit to wear, and a piece of dough partly permeated by the yeast. This process terminates in an eternal summer of perfection and glory. Believers have a beginning, they have and they have not, they possess and live in hope of possession. Luther used to quote James with special relish: "Of his own will he brought us forth by the word of truth, that we should be a kind of first-fruits of his creatures" (James 1:18). Between this beginning of the new creation and its completion lies a long road of divine ministration and human recovery.

Luther clearly never describes the life of the believer as static, as if it were merely oriented toward an inefficacious divine pronouncement. On the contrary, Luther with his hawk's eye for realities, views "the righteous and the sinner" in the concrete.

Of course, as we analyze these words, many questions bob up in our minds. What, for instance, is the meaning of the "simul"? How does it shape up concretely? Are we here reduced to a quantitative distribution of sinfulness and right-eousness, or are these words qualifications of the entire man? Again, have we here a two-fold aspect of a single unity, or a paradoxical anthropology?

Modern theologians have been put upon their mettle afresh by these questions. Of Luther's formula Van Niftrik, for instance, says: "Present-day theology has lost this Reformation insight into the nature of sanctification and the new life." Apparently, while all recognize residual sinfulness, the debate has shifted to the relation between the predicates "righteous" and "sinner" and their peculiar connection in simultaneity.

Warnings are afloat these days to the effect that the secret of
this simultaneity has been violated. The culprits are Kuyper
and Bavinck, over against Kohlbrugge, Böhl, and Barth, who
have once more revealed to us the true meaning of this formula.

The importance of these questions emerges also from the
consideration that even within the sphere of dialectical theology they are being debated. Brunner was not in the least
enthusiastic about Luther's phrase: "Luther's formula 'simul
peccator, simul justus' is as true as it is dangerous. In vain
do we look in the New Testament for it. What we read there
is that the law of the Spirit has made me free from the law of
sin and of death."[2]

It is important in regard to this dispute that Barth has rejected every quantitative interpretation of Luther's formula:
"The subject Sinner is not annulled by the predicate Righteous." He appeals to Luther's description of the believer:
"Flesh and spirit, sinner and righteous man, dead and freed
from death, guilty and not guilty,"[3] and adds, "and both to
the hilt and both at the same time. Let him that comprehends
this, comprehend it." The believer harbors a contradiction
as long as he lives. The victory over this "Widerspruch" can
never take place during his life "but is the act of the Word of
God, the act of Christ who is always the One who makes him
a sinner in order to make of this sinner a righteous man."
Barth knows of course that Luther also speaks of "in part
this, in part that" and of a residue of the old life; but these
expressions do not warrant the conclusion that Luther understood the relation between these two definitions in quantitative
terms. Some of Luther's formulations are susceptible of being
misunderstood, but, says Barth, they can never mean "that
the 'simul peccator et justus' resolves itself gradually more in

2. Emil Brunner, *Vom Werk des Heiligen Geistes,* 1937, page 57.
3. "Caro et spiritus, peccator et justus, mortuus et liberatus, reus et non
reus."

favor of the Justus in order to make room on the believer's deathbed for a completely redeemed Justus."[4]

We are dealing with qualifications of the whole man. Sin and grace are never mere "quanta" in process, grace increasing and sin decreasing. That, says Barth, is precisely the fatal scheme in the Catholic doctrine of grace and in the analogous doctrine of Schleiermacher. This quanta scheme would completely eclipse our serious condition. By means of this scheme St. Augustine paved the way for a refined semi-Pelagianism. Our situation is rather this, says Barth, not that our works are imperfectly obedient but that they are perfectly disobedient. There is no such thing as a gradual purification by which our need for the forgiveness of sins would diminish. Sinners we remain — completely; righteous we are through faith — again completely. Barth protests against the phrase "to miss the mark" because it leaves the impression that, with a fresh shot at obedience, we may undo our previous record.[5] In this manner we are fugitives from our status as sinners.

"I know of no other existence than that of sin and misery."[6] Barth is not averse to speaking of recuperation but that means, "from our human point of view, that we become sicker and sicker." Recuperation can only mean a search for justification. He cites Calvin who writes that "there never was an action performed by a pious man, which, if examined by the scrutinizing eye of Divine justice, would not deserve condemnation."[7]

This interpretation of Barth brings us to an important point. For Barth wishes to take account of the Reformed doctrine of man's total depravity. This doctrine, he says, is not invalidated by the justification of the sinner. Justification is not the elimination of sin; sin can only be forgiven. Man

---

4. Karl Barth, *Rechtfertigung und Heiligung.* 1927, in *Zwischen den Zeiten.*
5. Karl Barth, *De Apostolische Geloofsbelijdenis,* 1935, page 190.
6. Barth on Ludwig Feuerbach, *Zwischen den Zeiten,* 1927, page 37.
7. John Calvin, *Institutes,* III, 14, 11.

is man and never evolves into another kind of man. "The essence which we find peculiar to ourselves will always be one in hostility to God."[8]

* * *

These pronunciamentos of Barth, viewed in the light of his total dogmatics, do not necessarily indicate a grim disavowal of sanctification. Barth has set his jaws against any kind of infused grace as the basis for justification; but anyone who has read his discussions of the gratitude of God's children, will acknowledge that the issue Barth presents is not so much the fact as the nature of sanctification. Barth opposes especially the *habitus*-concept and denounces it as "the unbiblical conception of a supernatural qualification of the believer."[9]   He does, however, speak of "the being of man which is determined in faith through the Word and the Holy Spirit." Barth speaks of love and gratitude and wants to show that "it sustains an irreversible relationship to the love with which God loves us. Our love flows from and is grounded in his. Therefore, also, our love cannot justify us. How could it? Love is precisely our search for the Other who justifies us, as well as the acknowledgement that we cannot justify ourselves by what we are and do — not even by what we are and do as children of God."[10]   In this connection he writes further: "How could our love to God be inactive? It is all act, but wholly in the sense of a response of man to what God has told him. As such it is a work and has work," and, at the same time, "it is the surrender of all pretension and self-praise."[11]

There is an echo here of Calvin's opposition to "the erroneous notion of a partial righteousness,"[12] since our works are never — not even in part — the ground for our salvation. We can never, argues Calvin, "boast of I know not what frag-

---

8. Karl Barth, *Kirkliche Dogmatik*, II, 1, 1940, page 177.
9. *Ibid.*, I, 2, page 440.
10. *Ibid.*, page 441.
11. *Ibid.*, page 442.
12. John Calvin, *Institutes*, III, 14, 13.

ments of a few actions." With respect to the ground for our justification he is intransigent, as is Lord's Day 24: good works cannot even be a part of our righteousness. The point at issue then is the nature of the reality which, while it is appropriated by faith, is contained in Sovereign justification. How can we speak of this reality without doing injustice to Divine grace? The same Catechism, which denies us even a partial righteousness of our own, mentions the earnest purpose with which believers begin to live, not only according to all the commandments of God. It is this beginning which has its basis solely in justification by faith.

It is well to note that the Reformed Confessions never teach that believers, having gone through the gate of justification, now enter upon a new territory where they must, without outside help, take their sanctification in hand. It is not true that sanctification simply succeeds justification. Lord's Day 31, which discusses the keys of the kingdom, teaches that the kingdom is opened and shut by proclaiming "to believers, one and all, that, whenever they receive the promise of the gospel by a true faith, all their sins are really forgiven them." This "whenever" illustrates the continuing relevancy of the correlation between faith and justification. This correlation turned up before, namely, in the passage about the incipient obedience of the believer. The purpose of preaching the ten commandments, too, is that believers may "become the more earnest in seeking remission of sins and righteousness in Christ."[13] The Canons of Dort, in speaking of the perseverance of the saints, teach that God moves believers "to repentance, to a sincere and godly sorrow for their sins, that they may seek and obtain remission in the blood of the Mediator."[14]

Hence there is never a stretch along the way of salvation where justification drops out of sight.

---

13. *Heidelberg Catechism,* Question 115.
14. *Canons of Dort,* V, 7.

Genuine sanctification — let it be repeated — stands or falls with this continued orientation toward justification and the remission of sins. The fact that antinomianism was beaten down again and again with an appeal to the reality of sanctification resulted from listening attentively to the Word of God. But too often the bond between sanctification and Sola-fide was neglected and the impression was created that sanctification was the humanly operated successor to the divinely worked justification. The victim of this view can arrive only at a sanctification that is a causal process, and he is bound, in the end, to speak as Rome of an infused grace and of a quantitative sanctification.

Any reflection on sanctification will have to concentrate on the nature of the new beginning." This renewal of human life in gratitude and love has always been considered the work of the Holy Spirit. The Spirit alone could perform the miracle of making man walk on the road of sanctity without a sense of his own worth.

The history of dogma has witnessed a great deal of commotion about this miracle of the Spirit. We are thinking now of the so-called "gratia interna" and "gratia infusa." Rome, with its very pronounced doctrine of infused grace as infused sanctifying grace effecting a total transmutation, could not but stir up the pens of polemicists. Against this backdrop of Roman grace it is understandable that people became very diffident in approaching the reality of the renewal of life. For in the Roman doctrine of infused grace the correlation between faith and divine grace is entirely eclipsed: faith simply had to leave the field to make room for infused sacramental grace.

This fear of the Catholic doctrine of grace impelled people, at times, to dub as Catholic what has nothing to do with Catholicism. We are referring to the debate concerning regeneration. Especially the theology of Kuyper came on the carpet, but also the Canons of Dort were incriminated. These Canons treat, namely, of the new qualities "infused" into the will. Since this "habitus"-concept has been raked over the coals we must reflect on it. We are reminded of what Barth says concerning this concept of the later Calvinists: "Though the expression is not too fortunate, the thing intended is right."[15] What was this intended meaning?

The Canons point incontrovertibly to a change in human existence. One has merely to recall the following decisive formulation: "But by the efficacy of the same regenerating Spirit He pervades the inner recesses of man; He opens the closed and softens the hardened heart, and circumcises that which was uncircumcised; infuses new qualities into the will, which, though heretofore dead, He quickens; from being evil, disobedient, and refractory, he renders it good, obedient, and pliable; actuates and strengthens it, that like a good tree, it may bring forth the fruits of good actions."[16]

In full view here is the connection between the operation of the Holy Spirit and sanctification. Good works are spoken of as fruits of a good tree. It would be hard to maintain that the Canons view the believer in the light of his own achievements. Still it has been said that the Canons shunted from the true Reformed conception into a kind of Pietism, which is more interested in the regenerated man than in the grace of God. Further, people even sniffed the beginnings of a doctrine of physical, substantial grace when they read of qualities "infused" into the will. It seemed to them that the Canons had capitulated to the Catholic view of a mystical intrusion of a higher order of being. The Canons seemed to them to have too much of that "reality" of which the Reformation, according to Rome, had too little.

This criticism came especially from Böhl who debated warmly, on this point, with Kuyper. Böhl saw the doctrine of infused qualities as a threat to the central doctrine of the Reformation — that of justification by faith alone. This is the

15. Barth, *Kirkliche Dogmatik*, 1, 2, page 440.
16. *Canons of Dort*, III, IV, 11.

doctrine the fathers of Dort should have flung into the face
of Arminians; instead, in some evil hour, they thrust certain
qualities, and a quickened, sanctified will, in between man and
the Holy Spirit. Böhl does not maintain that justification
results in no change in man. To infer from his writings that
man remains unaltered, he says, is to nurse a malicious misunderstanding.[17] But the novelty in the life of the believer is
faith, not new qualities, or a "principle" of sanctification.
Böhl wishes to distinguish sharply between the qualities of
the will and the gifts of the Spirit. What is more, the gift
does not consist in new qualities but is the Holy Spirit himself.

These same motifs are operative in the polemics against
Kuyper. In Kuyper's theology, says Haitjema, regeneration
tends more and more to become a physical condition.[18] The
element of a change in substance is not clearly excluded from
his thinking. Proof in abundance is found, according to his
opponents, in Kuyper's terminology.

Recently Van Ruler offered a collection of terms he found
in Kuyper: infusion of new life, a new capacity, irradiation,
to plant a germ of life, new habits of will, the descent of
imperishable seed in the soil of our heart, to implant in our
innermost a new attitude, to change the innermost core of our
being. And the verbs are: to infuse, to irradiate, to increate,
to inculcate, to implant, to enter into, to descend into, to culti-
vate. These words are supposed to indicate the vast difference
between the Reformation and neo-Calvinism. They are the
criteria by which to judge whether modern Calvinists really
believe in justification by faith alone or whether they seek—
in line with Osiander — to find some essential righteousness
in man.

Honesty requires, however, that we be cautious in our
evaluation of the words used. Theological terms, like any

---

17. E. Böhl, *Von der Rechtfertigung durch den Glauben*, 1890, page 20.
18. Haitjema, *Karl Barth*, 1926, page 54.

other, must indeed be serviceable to the truths they are designed to convey. But let the critics rather search for the
writer's intent than peck away at his words.

Some theological honesty would help us to understand what
Kuyper means when he speaks of "seed" and "infusion." Does
not the Bible itself, when it talks about the work and the gift
of the Holy Spirit, use such expressions? We are thinking of
the "outpouring" of the Holy Spirit on Pentecost, of Paul's
teaching that "hope putteth not to shame, because the love of
God hath been *shed abroad* in our hearts through the Holy
Spirit" (Rom. 5:5), and of John's teaching that "whosoever
is begotten of God doeth no sin, because *his seed* abideth in
him: and he cannot sin, because he is begotten of God" (I
John 3:9).

These texts do not justify an unlimited use of imagery, it is
true; but they are nonetheless a warning against the simplistic
conclusion that such terms as Kuyper used must indicate a
physical grace.

All depends on whether it be understood that the operation
of the Holy Spirit is to us an inscrutable mystery. Of this
mystery the Scriptures speak in varying terms. Many admonitions, for instance, are based on the *indwelling* of the
Holy Spirit in the heart of believers (I Cor. 3:16). Paul
warns against sexual looseness in the same way: "Or know ye
not that your body is a temple of the Holy Spirit which is in
you, which ye have from God" (I Cor. 6:19). James contrasts the indwelling Spirit with the inclination to envy (James
4:5). The Scriptures also speak of God making his abode
with us (John 14:23), of the earnest of the Spirit in our
hearts (II Cor. 1:22), and of Christ dwelling in our hearts
through faith (Eph. 3:17).

It is undeniable that these texts have been used, in an in-
excusable fashion, to draw the Holy Spirit into a series of
dynamic causalities. People operated with the concept of
Christ *in us,* or the *Holy Spirit in us,* forgetting that the Holy

Spirit is God and that his Godhead is not in the least affected
by his indwelling. It will not do to speak of the work of the
Holy Spirit in human life, except with the greatest of rever-
ence and with an eye for its unique character. Let the reader
recall what the Canons of Dort say of the supernatural work
of the Holy Spirit, "most powerful and at the same time most
delightful, astonishing, mysterious, and ineffable." This "ineffable" should always stand out in our minds when we reflect
on the operation of the Holy Spirit in sanctification. Only
from this point of view will it be possible to enter into the debate concerning the "gratia infusa." The term itself, it is
said, compromises the exalted majesty of the Holy Spirit and
pushes into the foreground the inner change of man instead
of the grace of God.

Bavinck seems to leave himself wholly vulnerable when he
says that the Catholic doctrine of "gratia infusa" is not per se
wrong.[19] But he immediately adds: "The error is that Rome
made this infused righteousness the ground for forgiveness
and hence built religion on the foundation of morality. Believers do, however, become partakers of the righteousness
of Christ through infusion." To Bavinck, as well as to the
Canons, the concept of "infusion" was not necessarily Catholic. He did not want, from a reaction to Rome, to run the
danger of weakening the reality of sanctification. This cau-
tion did not prevent him from expressing sharp criticism of
the Roman doctrine of grace. Of this doctrine he says that
it completely alters the nature of grace, because grace is placed
in physical, instead of in ethical, antithesis to nature.[20] The
ethical contrast of sin and grace yields to that of nature and
super-nature.[21] Grace, according to Rome, is not first of all
the free favor of God in which He forgives our sins, but
a quality injected into man by which he shares, to some ex-

19. H. Bavinck, *Gereformeerde Dogmatiek*, IV, page 234.
20. *Ibid.*, II, page 505.
21. *Ibid.*, III, page 513.

tent, the divine nature. It is a supernatural, created, hyper-physical power — infused into man through the mediation of priest and sacrament — which elevates the recipient to the supernatural order.

Opposed to this view is the Reformed teaching that grace is the favor of God which relieves the believer of his sins for the sake of Christ. But this confession does not imply that the forgiveness would be a remote kind of righteousness in the sense that human life would not be enriched by it. Bavinck speaks also of grace as a power of God which enters into and alters human life. Ostensibly this view would correspond to the Catholic doctrine of grace, but the Reformers nonetheless meant something else.[22] The question is then: What is this "something else"? The discussion about God's work in man too often turns to man considered by himself. Man becomes the point of convergence for all kinds of forces and counter-forces and divine justification is lost to view. The work of the Holy Spirit in man must always be tied in with the orientation of man's faith to divine grace — an orientation which is effected by the Holy Spirit. The doctrine of the work of the Holy Spirit is designed precisely to prevent us from viewing man as an independent, dynamistic unit. This doctrine does not make man self-sufficient but rather underlines his perpetual and inherent lack of self-sufficiency. It was wedded indissolubly to the doctrine of the radical corruption of human nature. This corruption would preclude a living faith: flesh and blood and the powers of nature could not give birth to it. Hence the doctrine of the work of the Holy Spirit was an attempt to express the truth of Christ's teaching: "No man can come to me, except the Father that sent me *draw* him" (John 6:44), or, "Every one that hath heard from the Father, and hath *learned,* cometh unto me" (John 6:45), or, ". . . No man can come unto me, except it be *given* unto him

22. *Ibid.,* III, page 583.

of the Father" (John 6:65). If Bavinck and the Canons display interest in man, it is because they are interested in this truth of being drawn, of receiving, hearing and learning. Their concern is not man in his humanity and religious achievements but man as the Scriptures reveal him — in his inveterate alienation from God, in his enmity and blindness. It is noteworthy that the Canons discuss the work of the Holy Spirit and human depravity in the same chapter.

Once we have fully assimilated this fundamental point of view, we are ready to test every relevant formulation in its light. The prophet who has armed himself with this truth can confidently face the foe, be it mysticism, pietism, an unbalanced and warped interest in regenerate man, in short, any view that does less than justice to the all-determining righteousness and forgiveness that is of God. The believer's constant "commerce" with the forgiveness of sins and his continued dependence on it must — both in pastoral counselling and in dogmatic analysis — be laid bare, emphasized, and kept in sight. Only thus can we keep at bay the spectre of haughtiness — "as if we had made ourselves to differ."[23]

The dangers that beset us in our reflection on the work of the Holy Spirit cannot simply be evaded by means of a special theological technique. It is very well possible to speak about the Spirit's operations and still think only of man in his sinful self-containment. There is no rational technique that affords a priori insurance against anthropocentrism, nomism, and pharisaism. The only insurance known is an exultant faith which thrives on God alone and "forgets not all his benefits."

Communion with Christ through the Holy Spirit, and the sanctification which flows from their very nature, exclude the vainglorious concentration on man. Any religious autarchy whatever is vetoed by the truth of God's Word: "The people that are with thee are too many for me to give the Midianites into their hand, lest Israel vaunt themselves against me, say-

---

23. *Canons of Dort,* III, IV, 15.

ing, mine own hand hath saved me" (Judges 7:2). Only an unassuming faith can rightly speak about the "gratia interna" and the sovereign work of the Holy Spirit.

History shows how easy it is to get lost when one treats of internal grace. Osiander's views, the Catholic doctrine of infused grace, and any other conception which magnifies internal realities at the expense of the proclaimed Word of God, serve as ominous warnings.

Van Ruler, in speaking about internal grace, defends this term because it enables him, he says, to express the entrance of salvation into human existence. Internal grace is to him constitutive of the category of fulfilment; and he does not hesitate to speak of infused grace.[24] But neither does he give comfort to those who speak of grace as a substance. And he opposes especially those who assign to the mystical form of internal grace an absolute priority over its ethical form in the public life of man. The background of this fatal conception, according to Van Ruler, is a mystical anthropology in which all glory is given to "individual inwardness" — an anthropology evident in Catholic as well as in Reformed theology.

It is hard to see how Reformed theology can justly be charged with this fault. It has always protested vigorously against the Catholic "donum superadditum" as a new dimension in this sinful world. Regeneration and the Holy Spirit, as taught in the Confessions and by Kuyper, do not in the least warrant a withdrawal from the world of today. This thought enabled Kuyper to take a broad view of human life, to speak of the influence of the Gospel in it, and to teach the duties of believers toward it — even to the extent that he was saddled with the odium of having surrendered the sober mysteries of the Holy Spirit to the coarseness of a public salvation! Not inwardness versus a full human life is the issue presented by "gratia interna," but rather the renewal — through the sanctification of the believer — of all of human life. The doctrine

---

24. A. A. Van Ruler, *De Vervulling der Wet*, page 208.

of internal grace is a continual warning against the "hubris" of activism, against sanctification without forgiveness, against a "Christian" life without the Holy Spirit. What Van Ruler calls a "mystical" anthropology has always been rejected by Reformed theology because mysticism tended always to absolutize the "inner" man and to make it the hub of existence. Mysticism spoke of internal grace as if the adjective "internal" had swallowed up the noun "grace." Through the microscope of mysticism it is virtually impossible to see the sanctified *life* or even one's neighbor. In utter contrast with this minute concern with inwardness is the writing of Paul who, though he also treats of the Holy Spirit "which was given unto us" (Romans 5:5) glories in the cross of Christ by which the world is reconciled.

And he who would speak of the Holy Spirit in us in terms of the Scriptures will have to remain within that circle of light which the Word of God itself draws round the entire life of the believer in this world: "For by grace have ye been saved through faith; and that not of yourselves, it is the gift of God" (Eph. 2:8).

* * *

Our reflection on internal grace and the ineffable operation of the Spirit leads us to the mystery of the work of God. At best the Church of the ages gave but faltering expression to what needed to be said in the matter. Something it had to say to preserve the comfort and purity of the Gospel of grace; but those who tried to push beyond this ineffability soon lapsed into language that is hard, into formulas that are rigid, and into a matter-of-factness that is alien to the miracle of grace.

The Reformers, whenever they spoke of the work of the Holy Spirit in man, found themselves in sharp opposition to the Catholic views on this score, and tried especially to destroy the notion of the substantiality of internal grace. Grace, they emphatically taught, was not a "donum superadditum," a dimension or substance which served to complete man and made him an independent object of interest. With the "donum superadditum" they contrasted the biblical testimony which declares that grace is the favor and love of God which reconciles and redeems us unto himself. Bavinck, too, wrote in connection with the regenerating work of the Spirit: "The regenerate man is no whit different in substance from what he was before his regeneration." Grace must always — as here — be considered an act of the Holy Spirit and never abstracted from him. And when the Canons and Bavinck speak about "new qualities" and "gratia interna," they wish only to express the truth that the new life is not a product of flesh and blood. The judgment of charity would seem to be that theirs is a "theologia crucis" rather than a "theologia gloriae."

The idea in these admittedly imperfect formulations is certainly — as Böhl suggests — to interpose certain qualities between man and the Holy Spirit. The Canons deliberately mention the mysterious and ineffable operation of the Holy Spirit, and Bavinck, in his *"Roeping en Wedergeboorte,"* asserts that at the end of all our investigation we shall in all humility have to return to that sentiment of the Canons. All views which end up with some simplistic theory of regeneration will deprive us of the wonderful mystery of the work of the Holy Spirit — wonderful because it turns man from a study of his own condition to the life of faith in which he feeds on God's grace alone and seeks to continue in the sanctification he has received.

These same issues dogged the steps of Kuyper when, against all kinds of humanistic and semi-pelagian tendencies, he taught again that regeneration is an act of the Holy Spirit. This teaching governed all his thinking about regeneration. Not that such a starting-point would automatically exclude a critical analysis of his conceptions, but a failure to recognize it must certainly result in unfair evaluation. Kuyper was as little interested as Bavinck in a substantialist view of grace. And he wished to substitute the term "to declare righteous"

for "to make righteous." Over against the ethical theologies
he defended the forensic and declaratory character of justification.[25] In this connection he frequently indicated how not
to conceive the work of the Holy Spirit. He opposed the idea
that regeneration brings about any material change, and asserted that the word "seed" should only be used figuratively.
Sin is deprivation, a severing of the "umbiblical" cord between
the soul and God; hence regeneration can consist only in the
restoration of interrupted fellowship. Manicheism which regards sin as "a material deposit of venom"[26] was an abomina-
tion to Kuyper. The seed of regeneration, according to him,
is not "a germ of life or of holiness capable of being pointed
out." The seed of regeneration is, "in no respect, accessible
to the senses. It is purely spiritual." To neglect this truth is
to neglect the spiritual order. Kuyper did not hesitate to acknowledge that Böhl was absolutely right in protesting against
the subversion of this truth.

It is in the light of these facts that we must view Kuyper's
conception of internal grace and sanctification. He has labored like any other theologian to grasp the intent of the
Scriptures and to impress on his disciples that the work of
the Holy Spirit is, essentially, to cause the benediction of
God's grace to rest upon us.

In this connection he expressed himself, at times, in terms
which induced others to speak of his "theology of regeneration." They were moved to speak thus partly on the basis of
mistaken inferences and partly on the basis of formulations
which might rightly cause misgivings. Now and then Kuyper drew anthropological distinctions which are scarcely a
help in understanding the work of the Holy Spirit. He spoke,
for instance, about the "dual ego" — thinking thus to inter-
pret Romans 7:17: "So now it is no more I that do it, but
sin which dwelleth in me." The "I", according to Kuyper, is

25. A. Kuyper, E Voto II, page 334.
26. A. Kuyper, Het werk van den Heiligen Geest, page 401.

the hidden core of our personality. This innermost ego "was dead and has been made alive, was diseased and has been made healthy, lay under God's wrath and now basks in his favor, and is now utterly holy."[27] This hidden, innermost ego "is entirely holy and therefore sinless; it is indeed cut off from all sinfulness. It can no longer fall away, is inclined to all good and incapable of any evil. It is as sanctified as ever it will be in eternity." Sin is still present but no longer proceeds from man's innermost. The efforts of this sanctified ego are, regrettably enough, thwarted the moment they are directed outward into the world. At this point Kuyper calls in the aid of metaphor,[28] and tries to make intelligible how our innermost may be sinless while in our conscious life we must pray for the forgiveness of sins. For, says he, our hidden ego which is holy may enter into our conscious life in perverted fashion.

This approach of Kuyper to internal grace seems to us confusing. The fact that the believer once lay under God's wrath and now basks in his favor is here related to some duality in man, namely, that of center and circumference. This construction would seem to eclipse the good pleasure of God in justifying the wicked. Elsewhere Kuyper teaches a forensic justification which is *not* grounded in anything human, not even in a regenerated core. To speak thus synthetically about justification at the beginning and analytically at the end is a danger few are able to escape. For, by way of anthropological analysis, Kuyper arrives at a kind of Perfectionism — at least for the inner ego — and at the view that prayer for forgiveness is made necessary by the outer ego.

Regrettable, in this connection, is that many writers have confined their attention to formulations of this sort and explained Kuyper's theology entirely in their light. They did not understand that Kuyper wanted above all to maintain an antithesis over against any kind of merit in religion or sancti-

27. A. Kuyper, *Gemeene Gratie*, II, page 312.
28. *Ibid.*, pages 318-322.

fication. He wanted to maintain the reality of sanctification through faith and to point out, in opposition to all synergism, that even the very first beginning of the passage from darkness into light is possible and real only through the grace of God and by virtue of justification. The manner in which the Holy Spirit works cannot be completely understood by believers in this life. In fact, says Kuyper, we should steer clear of the attempt to explain this majestic act of God. But we must hold, on the basis of Scripture, to the reality of sanctification, even though we stand here at the borderline between life and death — a borderline which would be erased if anyone tried to explain regeneration from finite, human causes. And to oppose this heresy was Kuyper's chief endeavor. Regeneration, he taught, is an act of God by which the direction — not the substance — of human life is changed. When he tried to approach this truth anthropologically he lapsed into imagery which could not properly represent it; but however unsatisfying this treatment may be, it may not lead us to minimize the importance of an inquiry into the nature of the renewal by faith. This problem of the concrete renewal is very real — also for those who have stoutly opposed Kuyper's view of regeneration.

The opponents of Kuyper, having dealt with God's wrath and God's subsequent grace, must, as well as he, face the reality of the man who receives faith and continues in it: the believer whose ear of faith has heard the word of forgiveness and who now lives accordingly. The Confessions, both Lutheran and Reformed, mention the new obedience and the fruits of gratitude. The more fervent followers of Kohlbrugge did not always give an account of these cogent words and saw dangers which threw them too far in an opposite direction. Kohlbrugge himself did not hesitate at all to speak of a daily renewal, good works, and the fruits of righteousness. He wrote that the Spirit of the Lord "illumines our mind and sweetly bends our will to believe that we are one with the

Lord." When Kohlbrugge was asked whether the grace of God brought about a change in the relation between the sinner and God *as well as* a change in the heart of the believer, he replied affirmatively. Everywhere the same problem came to the fore. Bohl denied that justification left the sinner as he was and Van Niftrik doubted that Barth did justice to the fruits of the Spirit mentioned in Galatians 5. Woelderink said he had severe strictures against the doctrine of internal grace but did not in the least reject regeneration, conversion, faith and the obedience of faith. He is sharply at odds with Kuyper who, he says, capitulated to Rome in the matter of internal grace. But since he himself writes that conversion is not a natural process taking place in the hidden parts of the soul and that it issues from the Revelation through which, by the power of the Spirit, the living God still reveals himself, it appears that the debate concerning the work of the Spirit has not been fruitless and that there is practically a consensus among Reformed people. For Kuyper also wrote of the work of the Holy Spirit in terms of justification. The Holy Spirit communicates to us the benefits of Christ. And when Kuyper discusses the life-long battle of believers, he brings to the fore the temptations of the new life and the restless zeal with which Satan tries to push believers from the position they have taken in the Kingdom. That attack takes place now by way of seduction, now by playing on our most vulnerable point, then by throwing in our teeth our lack of faith or some ancient, long-forgiven sins. Against these temptations only patience offers resistance. We are admitted to the contest not, says Kuyper, because we have no accuser to bar our way but because in Christ we are acquitted of all our guilt and sins.[29] He does speak of wrestlers and a race-course. but anyone disposed to sniff at suggestion of strong men should read on about gentleness, meekness, patience, the Man of Sorrows, and Golgotha.

29. A. Kuyper, *Uit Het Woord,* second series III, page 345.

The important thing is that the work of the Holy Spirit be rightly related to the redemptive suffering and death of Christ. For this point is determinative — not such terms as internal grace, or infusion, or seed, or spark. These terms can be found in every theological work. no matter how divergent its theories. They do not necessarily indicate a "theology of regeneration." Haitjema was an opponent of Kuyper but he himself posits this question: "Is there in the soul of every natural man some slumbering spark of the higher life — a spark which needs only to be fanned into flame — or must that spark first be deposited in his heart by God's gracious revelation before there can be a life in fellowship with him?" This point of departure was Kuyper's as well. Witness his refusal to ascribe the wonderful transition from wrath to grace to any moral or religious disposition in man.

From this angle we shall be able to penetrate more deeply into the discussion about renewal — a discussion which can continue only if we free ourselves from every unsound dilemma. Lekkerkerker has written somewhere: "Only Kohlbrugge did justice to the fact that the new life of man in Christ is never a condition which would elevate him in anything above the unbeliever. The new life is Christ." He is especially averse to any confusion originating in the "Pietistic categories of being born again and not being born again." The theme of the Western church, he says, is: The controversy between a theology of justification and a theology of rebirth.

His view of this theme, however, is based on a false premise. It rightly reacts against dangerous tendencies in the doctrine of sanctification and against a conception of grace which, despite all its emphasis upon the initiative of divine grace, abstracted sanctification from faith and justification. But it is nonetheless unacceptable, because it makes an either-or proposition of God's verdict of acquittal and the Spirit's act of renewal. Not the categories of rebirth and non-rebirth

are Pietistic but rather an abstracted rebirth in which man
supposedly receives qualities which elevate him above others.
Such a view, however, is a perversion of that internal grace
which always allows the work of the Spirit to be founded,
through faith, upon the forgiveness of sins: and any sanctification whatever must spring from this forgiveness.   The renewal is not a mere supplement, an appendage, to the salvation given in justification.   The heart of sanctification is the
life which feeds on this justification.   There is no contrast between justification as act of God and sanctification as act of
man.   The fact that Christ is our sanctification is not exclusive of, but inclusive of, a faith which clings to him alone in
all of life.   Faith is the pivot on which everything revolves.
Faith, though not itself creative, preserves us from autonomous self-sanctification and moralism.

The Canons of Dort have viewed the life of believers so
enthusiastically as a gift that they spoke of a transition from
death into life.   They asserted that the Scriptures highly
extol rebirth, renewal, new creation, and the resurrection from
the dead.   This ineffable act of the Spirit is said to be "not
inferior in efficacy to creation or the resurrection from the
dead."[30]   In the articles about human corruption there is
strong and consistent reference to the shift in man from trusting in himself to trusting in the grace of God alone.   Very
concretely the Canons treat of the efficacy by which the regenerating Spirit pervades the inmost recesses of man.[31]   It
must be remembered that the Canons here contradict the
Arminian concept of "moral suasion."   In the rejection of
errors the Canons again take issue with those who teach "that
in the true conversion of man no new qualities, powers, or gifts
can be infused by God into the will."[32]   The Canons — this
much is apparent — shy away from a pschology of conversion

30. *Canons of Dort*, III, IV, 12.
31. *Ibid.*, 11.
32. *Ibid.*, rejection of errors, 6.

or an ontology of grace but make an effort not to ascribe any
credit for man's renewal to himself and to depict the life that
rests on grace alone. Faith, the Canons immediately add, is
not first of all an act but a gift.

The point is to give religious expression to the nature and
origin of faith. The hard heart is softened and the closed
heart opened. The powerful operation of God must be understood in connection with the refusal to view grace as "a gentle
advising," which is not sufficient to make the natural man
spiritual.[33] Instead of such powerless persuasion, the Canons
teach another and far more powerful and divine manner of
the Holy Spirit's working in the conversion of man.

The Canons do not sanction a particular psychology but
they bring to light the miracle of the Holy Spirit as evident
in the faith of the sinner. God does not merely illuminate the
mind of believers — confront them with new data — but
powerfully changes heart and will. No man may infer from
the Canons a settled anthropology, but we may read here a confession of a divine grace which precipitates a total renewal.

For this reason, too, Reformed theology has always been at
sixes and sevens with Amyraldism which placed all emphasis
upon the illumination of the mind. Over against this one-
sided and erroneous view, the composes of the Canons were
convinced that being made alive implied a radical turn-about:
a transformation from an apostate pseudo independence to a
meek and active faith in God's mercy.

Intelligible at this point also is the association of regeneration and faith. Faith, according to Article 24 of the Belgic
Confession, is "wrought in man by the hearing of the Word
of God and the operation of the Holy Spirit"; and this utterance is the preface to an article about man's sanctification and
good works. It is the aim of this Confession to relate the
totality of human life to divine grace, and therefore our fathers
tried, in their terminology of faith, rebirth, and new creation

---

33. *Ibid.*, rejection of errors, 7.

to indicate the deep-rootedness and priority of grace, thus to exclude, a la John Calvin, any hint of a meritorious transition. These terms did not generally provoke any talk of a "theology of regeneration." This approach came later, when the distinction arose between regeneration in a narrower and a wider sense, and when regeneration was spoken of as beginning of new life. At this juncture people suspected the entrance of a Pietistic theology which drew more attention than is warranted to an "empirical" change in the human heart. Some feared that this distinction was more than academic and that it imperilled the correlation between faith and sanctification.

Bavinck has pointed out that this change in terminology was readily assimilated so that today hardly a soul seems to associate regeneration with sanctification. He explains this phenomenon by saying that the word "rebirth" quite logically makes us think of the coming into existence of the new life. But he acknowledges that theology has assigned a narrower meaning to the word than has the Bible.

When in connection with the baptism and early death of children the possibility was broached of regeneration before faith and conversion, this sentiment gained strength, according to Bavinck, "from the consideration that the moment faith and conversion are seen to flourish amid the corruption of human nature, it is natural to trace them to an antecedent, interior operation of the Spirit." Regeneration and conversion need, at least logically, to be distinguished and to be placed in the given order. Bavinck obviously does not, in this utterance, subscribe to a temporal succession; and it seems to us it had been better to speak of a religious succession, since the issue is, at bottom, the antecedence of divine grace.

Bavinck rightly brings out that, in Methodism, Pietism, and Rationalism, the relation between regeneration and faith has been inverted, since man was said to be called to the moral act of faith and conversion. "By that faith he was regenerated and his life improved." Hence here regeneration ensues upon the act of faith and the priority of grace is lost to view, whereas in the post-Reformation change in terminology there is the sustained effort to maintain this priority throughout the process of salvation.

This effort is very pronounced in Kuyper. His primary concern is that the gracious work of the Holy Spirit be never deduced from anything in man, since such deduction would be in hopeless conflict with the nature of faith. The acceptance of salvation must never be understood as a contribution to the realization of that salvation. Therefore Kuyper calls the idea of moral persuasion a "grating perversion of the truth by which the glorious origin of the new life was obscured."[34]

It is self-evident that any view of regeneration, faith, and sanctification, must be weighed and tested by the criterion of whether it does justice to the forgiveness of sins as the only ground and source of sanctification. This is the truth preached by the Belgic Confession (Article 24) when it says that it is faith which regenerates man and causes him to live a new life. This, too, is the reason why the Canons oppose the overestimate of faith which would make it a condition for, and the achievement of, the reception of salvation. Faith simply and finally excludes human merit and understands that we are drawn by the power of the Holy Spirit to a living fellowship with our Lord.

Only thus — and thus only — may we speak of the beginning of sanctification. It is necessary always to refurbish these truths in the face of so much anxiety lest internal grace should become for us a property independent of — at least partially — the grace that is from above, and in the face of so much indifference to this danger.

Shunning all one-sidedness and steering clear of all besetting heresies, we must cling through faith to God's grace alone. Then we shall be able to do justice to the real beginning of sanctification: the regeneration by faith of which Cal-

---

34. A. Kuyper, *Het Werk van den Heiligen Geest*, page 381.

vin and the Confessions speak. Intimately related to these as-
sertions is what the Heidelberg Catechism says about the word
"beginning." For here the beginning covers the entire lives
of believers on earth. "Even the holiest men, while in this
life, have only a small *beginning* of this obedience; yet . . .they
began to live . . . according to all the commandments of God.[35]

Thus the church spoke about sanctification and proclaimed
at the same time this eschatological prospect: ". . . till after
this life we arrive at the goal of perfection."[35] If we now proceed to discuss the progress of sanctification, it is certainly not
our wish to reach out beyond this "beginning." But our reflection on sanctification must also include its progress, for
here, too, the true nature of sanctification and renewal may be
obscured and the vision of Sola-gratia denied to us.

_____

95. Lord's Day 11.

The Progress of Sanctification

CHAPTER V

The Progress of Sanctification

ALTHOUGH there is no essential difference in meaning between the word "progress" and the word "process," the last-mentioned always seemed to include some evolutionistic element. The problem we confront here is not simplified by the word "progress" but it indicates at least that we are now concerned with the life of believers: the life which is in motion from day to day, in progress on the way of salvation. Anything which can be said about the beginning and progress of sanctification is conditioned by the nature of this salvation. Hence we must raise the question: What is the nature of this progress? In what kind of motion is the believer involved on his way to the goal of perfection?

It is beyond dispute that the Bible itself treats of this progress. Many admonitions point to a required "movement." We are exhorted to perfect our holiness in the fear of God (II Cor 7:1), to following after the sanctification without which no man shall see the Lord (Heb. 12:14), to follow after that which is good (I Thess. 5:15), after love (I Cor. 14:1), after righteousness, godliness, faith, love, patience, and meekness (I Tim. 6:11). Everything points to consistent and active endeavor.

We read also of growing in the grace and knowledge of our Lord and Savior Jesus Christ (II Peter 3:18), and Paul makes the strong assertion that the faith of the Thessalonians "groweth exceedingly, and the love of each one of you all toward one another aboundeth" (II Thess. 1:3).

When the Bible speaks thus about progress and being holy "in all manner of living" (I Peter 1:15), we are struck by the simplicity of these admonitions. Under the influence of many discussions we run into the danger of taking such words as "growing" and "increasing" as indicative of measurable magnitudes, and soon we think of moralistic improvement. It is all the more necessary, therefore, to scrutinize the Scriptures about the progress of sanctification. The Confessions also speak with clarity in the matter. They mention the "more and more" of sanctification. In Lord's Day 44 we read of being renewed more and more after the image of God and in Lord's Day 48 of submitting more and more to the Lord. The Belgic Confession (Article 24) speaks not "of a vain faith but of such a faith which is called in Scripture a faith working through love, which excites man to the practice of those works which God has commanded in his word." And the Canons, to complete the picture, exhort us "to mortify the flesh more and more."

What accounts for all the debate, especially that concerning the progress of sanctification? The answer is not difficult. The same anxiety we saw in connection with the beginning of sanctification and internal grace returns to us, if possible, with increased force. The word "striving" has enough emotional color to indicate our problem. The nature of this striving as implicit in the progress of sanctification became a scorching-hot issue when the church, averse as it was to any nomistic striving and "work-righteousness," tried to tear it from its bosom.

Again we stand amid the fierce debates revolving round the figure of Kohlbrugge. It was he who gave utterance, throughout his life, to his concern lest some sort of moralism should crowd out the comfort of salvation. Against all the moralistic tendencies of his day he sounded a clear protest and tried to lead the people back to the evangelical message of radical justification: Sola-fide.

The emphasis with which he spoke tended, in the course of his development, to become stronger in proportion to the opposition he faced. Dominating the debate was his sermon on Romans 7:14. And one of the charges against him was that of Antinomianism. Even Krummacher though that he had tasted the heady poison of this heresy when Kohlbrugge asserted, among other things, that he had authority "even in the midst of sin to glory in the righteousness of Christ." Kohlbrugge was accused in this debate, in which he fought against a wrong view of sanctification, of violating also the right view. Da Costa said he could not conceive a greater distance than that existing between Kohlbrugge's doctrine and the triple knowledge of the Catechism: sin, redemption, and gratitude. He reminds Kohlbrugge that Christ does not sit idly by but works in us a life of sanctification. He accuses him of going no further than the truth that "God is for us" and neglecting the law of liberty. In the sermon of Romans 7:14 he finds no mention of the work of the Holy Spirit. The idea of a "vicarious sanctification" is to him a self-contraction.

Kohlbrugge was deeply scandalized by this criticism. Had he not read all the antinomian literature he could lay his hands on, only to thank God he had been spared this horrid heresy? Da Costa may know that he considers Antinomians a loathsome sect and their doctrine the excrement of hell. Kohlbrugge points out that the doctrine of gratitude receives a ready welcome in his scheme: he too believes that the will of God is to follow holiness. But he denies that it is necessary to speak separately of sanctification, once the doctrine of the righteousness of Christ and of grace has been understood. His worry is that of the Belgic Confession (Article 24): "Our consciences would be continually vexed if they relied not on the merits of the suffering and death of our Savior." To forget this truth is to end in a morass of moralism and to assign to the law a function it does not have. "Throw away the crutches of your righteousness," says Kohlbrugge, "throw them far from you! With them it is impossible to climb the mount of the Lord. Tear those rags from you with which you are trying to cover your wounds, and appear before the Righteous and Holy One just as you are! Before Him to despair of self is salvation." To rely on the righteousness of Christ is the beginning and the end. The believer will never invalidate the confession of Paul: "I am carnal" — "carnal in body and soul, in mind and will, in all my senses and members. My total existence is sin, but through faith I am partaker of the full righteousness and holiness of Christ." In registering his protest against a legalistic sanctification Kohlbrugge uttered these words — also a source of much discussion: "The law is for us a corpse which we have rightly buried." And he adds: "We also have become corpses to the law, since it has become dead to us, and we have no further truck or trade with it after we have become Christ's." Acidly he exposes the pious devil who would let men perform all sorts of devout works for the sake of killing their members. For this "process" Kohlbrugge has only scorn. Let no one think, he says, that the old man is killed any more at fifty than at twenty. Gradually to overcome sin is a mirage, a futile endeavor, and serves only the indulgence of the flesh. With special affection he points to the verb form Paul uses in Colossians 3:5, and says it should read: "Have put to death, therefore, your members which are upon the earth," instead of "Put to death. . . ."

Sanctification is not a "process," certainly not a moral process, but it is being holy in Christ and having part, through faith, in his righteousness. The imperative of Paul is identical with: Believe! All depends on Christ. "Once I have Christ I need no longer worry about my sanctification, no, but I press on and count all things to be loss for the excellency of the knowledge of Christ Jesus my Lord." Expressions such as these were provocative. The opponents of Kohlbrugge were not sufficiently conscious, however, of his passionate reaction against all legalistic holiness and his eagerness to warn against it. Kohlbrugge could never shake himself free from what Paul says about the law. But he was unflagging also in his emphasis on the significance of the decalogue and in his praise of the third part of the Catechism.

However great the difference may be between the theology of Barth and Kohlbrugge, there is a common motif which explains the sympathy with which Barth regards Kohlbrugge. Barth's opposition to the subjectivistic theology of the nineteenth century brought him in the vicinity of Kohlbrugge who, against the tenor of the times, witnessed powerfully to justification. Barth protested also against the devout, self-assured Christian, against his pretensions, his positiveness, and vitality. This man is a fugitive from grace and takes his life into his own hands. His criticism was directed against a "theology of grace" which permitted the sinner, on the basis of grace, to function in building a new order, an order of his own, by which the kingdom of God was thought to come.

Both Barth and Kohlbrugge spurned justification as a gateway to sanctification as well as a sanctification which made the justification of the ungodly unnecessary. Thus, from all directions, it seemed to Barth, actual grace was violated; and the fact that there is no other difference between the church and the world than that the church does know and the world does not know its wickedness was denied.

Haitjema compared Kohlbrugge's sermon on Romans 7:14 with the radical change of front apparent in the Römerbrief of Barth, and spoke of a shift to "the criticism of faith." If he meant that sanctification is always related to faith, no Reformed man will dispute it, for the Confessions are unequivocally certain of the bond between faith and good works. This bond was sometimes forgotten, however, and on this account Kohlbrugge reacted with such violence. It is no wonder that Kohlbrugge was so inhospitable toward the criticism of Da Costa. For Da Costa, whose exegesis of I Cor. 1:30 ("Christ was made unto us righteousness and sanctification") amounted to saying simply that Christ is for us and in us, failed utterly to take faith into account. When he says that Christ works

in us, he leaves the impression that good works follow merely
— as from some sort of dynamic causality according to the
law of cause and effect — from the fact of faith. But the relation between faith and sanctification is unique: faith is not a
fact producing other facts but it is dependence on the grace
of God and not to be thought of apart from its object. Kohlbrugge's accentuation of Sola-fide, in opposition to Da Costa,
was certainly warranted. By this token he followed in the
tracks of Calvin and Luther who taught that we are justified,
not by love, but by faith.

Haitjema, however, accompanied the Reformed view of
these matters with his rejection of any idea of process. To
him there are two alternatives: "Either sanctification as being
holy through the spirit of faith, or sanctification as a process,
a becoming holy through the indwelling operation of the Holy
Spirit." Hence the alternatives are "being through faith" and
"becoming." Having made allowance for Haitjema's reaction
against the idea of an independent process, we must nonetheless assert that neither Scripture nor the Confessions will
countenance this dilemma. The fact that the "becoming" is
so often given a nomistic interpretation may not lead us into
that trap. We must track down the nature of the "progress"
which is not in conflict with the "being" but inseparable from
it. Is there no progress in which the believer, rather than
sweating out his own good works and cultivating his own
regeneracy, relies more and more on the grace of God? Since
Haitjema would reply affirmatively, there is no good reason
for connecting the central question of sanctification with his
dilemma.

There is in Kohlbrugge's view, as Haitjema himself admits,
a tendency toward passivity and some of his followers have
drawn their own unfortunate conclusions. The cause appears
to lie in the fact that the progress of sanctification is too often
approached with prejudices aroused by the legalistic striving
after holiness. Hence people shrank back even from the "more

and more" of Scripture and Confessions, and especially the disciples of Kohlbrugge began to speak about sanctification with unnecessary and unnatural fear, reacting as they were against a so-called "ontology" of grace.

Kohlbrugge — according to Haitjema — did, in his later life, speak of a progressive sanctification and claimed that this concept was not a denial of the views he had always championed. We agree wholeheartedly that progressive sanctification is compatible with a faith-connected sanctification. A deflection from a properly related justification and sanctification exists only in the view that faith — as an isolated function — is the cause of good works. Anyone who manages to maintain the full status of Sola-fide can speak about progressive sanctification without stumbling into the pit of legalism. If only Kohlbrugge and his followers had given more explicit expression to this religious motif they could have meant more to people like Da Costa whose too simple view of sanctification precluded his seeing the nexus between Gospel and faith, faith and good works, faith and the law of God.

To the man who understands that a progressive sanctification must keep the windows of faith opened to the grace of God, the surprising multiformity of the Word of God will be intelligible. For one moment we are directed to follow after holiness and another to grow in the grace and knowledge of Jesus Christ. This multiformity preserves us both from passivity and from nomism. Any "striving," in this connection, receives its content from the fact of grace. Not activity as such is disqualified by Scripture but only the activity which cannot be considered as a growing in grace or as the perfection of holiness in the fear of God.

The progress that is here meant is like the fruitbearing of branches in the vine. The branch, if broken from the vine, cannot bear fruit. "So neither can ye, except ye abide in me." "He that abideth in me, and I in him, the same beareth much fruit: for apart from me ye can do nothing."

Abiding in him — united with him because of the words which "abide in you" — all this points to communion by faith. From this communion flow the fruits. And the disciples are called upon to bear these fruits. That is the call to action. But not a fleck of self-impelled action remains. It is *the man of God* who must flee from sin (I Tim. 6:11), and the Lord's *servant* who must not strive (II Tim. 2:24). The *beloved* of the Lord are told: "But ye, beloved, building up yourselves on your most holy faith, praying in the Holy Spirit, keep yourselves in the love of God, looking for the mercy of our Lord Jesus Christ" (Jude 20, 21).

All activity and progress must bear this stamp. Progress is opposed to all evil and deceit, all pretence, and jealousy, and slander. Believers must be eager, like new-born babies in God's family, for the unadulterated spiritual milk of God's Word, if they have tasted that the Lord is gracious (I Peter 2:1-3), that they may grow unto salvation. For this activity of faith is not alien to being employed as living stones in the construction of a spiritual house (I Peter 2:3), and thus to be a holy priesthood.

In the announcement of salvation, and the warning which is implicit in it, lies the death-warrant for all nomism. Woe unto the moralistic toiler who should forget the heart of Peter's sermon: You "who in time past were no people, but now are the people of God: who had not obtained mercy, but now have obtained mercy" (I Peter 2:10).

Between Romans 1-11 and Romans 12 there is therefore the most intimate harmony, as also between Hebrews 1-12 and Hebrews 13. Nowhere can we find a break between justification and sanctification. There is only the relationship in which the grace of God admonishes the progressing believer. The proclamation of God's grace which preceded the admonition is never neglected in the admonition but rather applied, and given content, in it.

In the very midst of the admonitions of Hebrews 13 comes the assurance that Jesus Christ is always the same (Heb. 13:8), and that it is good for the heart to be established by grace (Heb. 13:9). The redemptive work of Jesus Christ of which the epistle is full is never out of sight: amidst the exhortations is an altar and the Man of Sorrows suffering without the gate (Heb. 13:12), "that he might sanctify his people." All the admonitions about brotherly love and hospitality, about concern for prisoners and the purity of married life, find their point of gravity in the continual sacrifice of praise to God and in confessing his Name (Heb. 13:15). The golden ring which encloses all of sanctification is shut with the words: "Grace be with you all" (Heb. 13:25).

It cannot be denied that grace is the dominant motif in all admonition. The night is far spent, and the day is at hand. Therefore let us cast off the works of darkness and put on the armor of light (Romans 13:12).

All this is decisive for the progress of sanctification. By clinging closely to these truths we shall be able to distinguish genuine progress from every movement cut loose from the anchorage of faith. This progress has been described very accurately in Lord's Day 44 where the significance of preaching the law is set forth in its bearings on the life of sanctification. We note four elements:

1. Increasing knowledge of our sinful nature.

2. Increasing earnestness in seeking remission of sin and the righteousness of Christ.

3. Prayer to God for the grace of the Holy Spirit and a constant endeavor to be renewed more and more after the image of God.

4. The eschatological prospect: the goal of perfection.

Every element in this description is important. The "more and more" is wrapped up in seeking remission of sin through the righteousness of Christ, in the prayer for grace and in looking forward to the future. How remote this is from any moralistic sanctification!

This Lord's Day is a vivid reminder of the Scriptures which tell of the earnest of the Spirit given us in our hearts (I Cor. 1:22), and of the Holy Spirit as earnest of the inheritance (Eph. 1:14). The assumption beneath this eschatological perspective is, of course, the reality of communion through the Holy Spirit, but at the same time Paul emphasizes the fact of unfulfilment and anticipation. We have, says Paul, the first-fruits of the Spirit and therefore we groan within ourselves, waiting for our adoption, to wit, the redemption of our body (Rom. 8:23). These first-fruits reveal to us the partial and temporary nature of our present condition. The adoption of the future is not a denial of the adoption of the present; the two are twins. Believers must shine as lights precisely in their quality of children. Sanctification reveals itself, both in the adoption and in the growing awareness of sonship, as the renewal after the image of God.

In 1930 Barth wrote about the eschatological sonship of believers. In this connection, he viewed as black error the teaching of Augustine that man himself, through the infusion of righteousness, becomes the bearer of salvation.[1] Hence he stressed both the divine presence and its eschatological nature. The synthesis by which he managed to exclude the presence of the Holy Spirit as a Conditioner of human life was that the reality of the eschatological presence exists in the promise. "Our divine future, the final gift which God has willed for us, exists in the present through the Word."[2] Our regeneration and adoption must be understood unreservedly as eschatological entities. Barth protests sharply against reducing the biblical relationships to mere anthropological distinctions, in order, finally, to make them the objects of a Christian psychology. "All must remain implicit in the Word . . . and therefore is

1. Karl Barth, *Der Heilige Geist und das Christliche Leben*, page 95.
2. *Ibid.*, page 97.

not in our possession, not in the fleshly tentacles of our rational or irrational modes of experience."

But this choice of alternatives is hardly Scriptural. The enemy Barth is here opposing is a caricature. It is hard to see why the actual presence of the Holy Spirit in the church, a reality we can know only through faith, must necessarily imply a reduction to human levels. The distinction between the Holy Spirit and our spirit will never, not in all eternity, be annulled. Nor is it annulled in the present. Barth imagines his opponent to be someone who in reaching out impatiently for future realities tries to push beyond the word of promise. But the Reformed view of beginning and consummation, the first-fruits and the full harvest, is not impatient: it wishes merely to acknowledge that the gift of the Spirit dwells among us today. It is this gift which makes us long for the coming of the Lord. The false option which Barth entertains misled him into viewing the adoption solely in terms of the future. He arrives at this juncture by manipulating the concept "promise." "Who is grateful to God? Who is a free child of God? I have not said: there are such people; nor: the Christian just *is* grateful and *has* the freedom of the children of God. That would be Augustinian doctrine again, even if dressed up in Protestant finery."[3]

It is undeniable that the Scriptures speak differently about the adoption to sonship. Paul does indeed refer to the adoption as an eschatological reality (Romans 8:32), but he speaks no less about the reception of the Spirit of adoption by which we cry: Abba, Father. That Spirit bears witness with our Spirit that we are children of God (Romans 8:15, 16). The answer to Barth's thesis that "all must remain implicit in the Word" is that the secret of the adoption is implicit in these words and in the testimony of the Holy Spirit, so that there

---

3. *Ibid.*, page 103.

can be no talk of a contradiction between promise and fulfilment. The idiom of faith, in these matters, is so simple. John says, speaking about the future: "Beloved, now are we children of God, and it is not yet made manifest what we shall be" (I John 3:2). John points out, as it were, the riches of the present.

This reality of sonship is in contrast with the righteousness of works. For the secret of this sonship lies in the acknowledgement of grace. All progress in sanctification moves within the boundaries of being sons of the Father. This progress is not an automatic, causal development from first-fruits to full harvest but a progression in faith, prayer, meekness, and confession of guilt. The "more and more" is applicable only if kept within the bounds of sonship.

The progress of sanctification, therefore, is a process comparable with no other process. Too often analogies and metaphors have done violence to its unique character. For progress in sanctification never meant working out one's own salvation under one's own auspices; on the contrary, it meant working out one's own salvation with a rising sense of dependence on God's grace. Anyone who thinks that this delimitation would compel us to pay but sparing attention to this life has not penetrated to the depths of the biblical message of grace. This life, this world, cannot be abstracted from our being dependent sons of the Father. This life — the Christian life, that is — can only be the manifestation of our sonship. Thus we can understand that progress in sanctification can never consist in building up ourselves on our morality. Litanies of guilt are spoken on the way of salvation, not only during the first stage of conversion, but, as Christ becomes more wonderful to us, in crescendo.

The debate concerning the nature of sanctification has never been exclusively theological. Ties with common, everyday life have never been severed. Sanctification concerns this life

from start to finish.   And the question rises in us: Is there
in this progress, growth, and transition also a growth in self-
consciousness, in power, in the conscious life before God and
man?   Our confession leaves room only for "a small beginning," even for the saintliest soul, throughout the process of
sanctification.

It is well that — before going further — we reflect on the
relation between sanctification and humility.

Sanctification and Humility

CHAPTER VI

Sanctification and Humility

KUYPER has pointed out that a simple, evolutionistic doctrine of sanctification can never be harmonized with an increasing sense of guilt.[1] "This phenomenon would be unthinkable. Such a process would rather diminish the devout man's sense of guilt." Instead we must have "the simultaneous growth of sanctification and the consciousness of sin." This is an enigma, says Kuyper, which can be resolved only by the words of Christ: "If any man would follow me, let him deny himself."

The question we face now is how to find our bearings with regard to this riddle. The answer to this question determines whether we shall have a true or a spurious sanctification. It touches the heart of the Confessions.

For if anything is clear in the message of Scripture, it is that in sanctification there is never, under any circumstances, any room for self-pride or self-praise. This apparent truism may not blind our eyes to the dangers which threaten, especially at this point, to turn sanctification into its opposite. It will become apparent that it is the Scripture-taught relation between faith and sanctification which excludes the possibility of self-admiration.

The aspect of self-praise, "self-consciousness," and self-conceit, is a recurrent element in the debates touching sanctification. Barth and Kohlbrugge did not cease to register their protest against self-praise: not first of all that of the self-sufficient, autonomous man of humanism, but that of the Chris-

---

1. Abraham Kuyper, *Uit het Woord*, first series I, page 219.

tian. From the days of his Römerbrief Barth warned against
Christian positiveness by which, on the supposed basis of
grace, the grace of God was in fact dethroned in self-righteousness. During this early period Barth fulminated with great
vehemence against the church and its pretensions: The church
is the grave of biblical truth. She has crucified the Christ
afresh. The way of the church and the way of Christ are
henceforth two divergent ways.[2] His blasts were funnelled
especially toward the religious man, the *beati spossidentes*
(those possessing blessedness), who distinguished themselves
from, and elevated themselves above, the world. His wrath
was kindled against satedness, against pharisaism, against the
sense of having arrived. In this atmosphere the "realities" of
the present would completely overshadow the glory of the last
days. This protest remains to this day one of the main elements in Barth's polemics and was shot particularly at the
Catholic Church, which he called "the most outstanding form
of this de-eschatologized Christianity."[3] In the same vein
Kohlbrugge warned insistently against the exaggerated self-
confidence of the devout man who is, unwittingly, a fugitive
from his status as ungodly man, awaiting there and thus to be
justified.

It is to be expected that this protest, like any other, is subject to becoming one-sided and trite, and that possibly the cry
against pharisaism is raised in places where it does not exist.

But however easily the condemnation of Pharisaism may
degenerate, it is impossible to deny the great significance of
the Scriptural warning against self-praise and self-elevation.
This warning springs not from a critical spirit but from the
Gospel itself. We must never forget that the sin of Pharisaism
arose in intimate connection with religion, the religion of the
law of God. The Pharisees cherished the thora as the blueprint of their lives but, it is clear, never understood the thora.

---

2. Karl Barth, *Römerbrief*, page 314.
3. Karl Barth, *Kirchliche Dogmatik* III, 2, 1948, page 615.

The law of God held no terror for them. They imagined their lives to be flawless. This familiarity with the law of the Holy One finally warped their entire attitude toward the grace of God and toward Jesus Christ whom they condemned and crucified. By this route we arrive at hypocrisy, the leaven of the Pharisees.

This hypocrisy infected their prayer, their fasting, their almsgiving; it smothered mercy; it perverted their view of life; it made them look for their reward among men. In their religion the Pharisees would be seen of men: theirs was the caricature of shining as lights in the world. Thus they made void the Word of God. Of them Isaiah prophesied: "This people honoreth me with their lips: but their heart is far from me" (Matt. 15:8). The doctrines of the Pharisees were a masquerade which hid the stark unbelief of their hearts. Their piety is sham even in their boundless admiration for the law; for they had lifted the law from the context of the Covenant of Grace and made it a part of the total complex of stipulations which had to be carried out.

In their own way the Pharisees had found a solution for the problem of separation. The Pharisees owed their name to their dedication to the separated life among the people of Israel, which owed its very existence to the separation and sanctification originating in God. The sect of the Pharisees is living proof of how this sanctification and separation may be misunderstood and perverted. This degeneracy is at the heart of their proclamation of an antithesis between them and the people of the land. In their isolation they would dissociate themselves from all impurity; they despise Jesus for dining with publicans and sinners. Since they had abstracted the law from the Gospel, they could not but regard religion in terms of merit, and so the Pharisee in the parable speaks of himself five times, unlike the publican who mentions himself once and then as an object of mercy. The Pharisee is presented as grateful: Lord, I thank thee (Luke 18:11). Apparently gratitude has a place in the pharisaic religion but actually it is a meaningless concept in the mouth of a Pharisee. For that's how they are, the children of hell, in spite of and even in their missionary zeal.

That's how they are, those who trust in themselves that they are righteous (Luke 18:9) and who have no need to be justified of God. Their attitude to life, viewed from the religious angle, is that of the apostate. They allowed God a place in their lives and actually thought they did him a service. From this nomistic religion flowed the self-consciousness which made the Pharisee look down his supercilious nose at others (Luke 18:11).

This pharisaism embodies a degenerate sanctification which arises from breaking the bond between faith and sanctification. It does not imply a rejection of the existence of God, and unbelief in that sense, but it implies that their faith was not riveted upon divine grace and divine justification. Therefore their striving after holiness became vain and destructive of true religion.

This danger is not merely historical: it besets the church always. Because sanctification summons us in a particular way to activity and endeavor, all this activity is under the constant scrutiny of the divine Judge.

This permanent danger to the church may preoccupy us with such force that we may be moved to deny the existence of any distinction between believer and unbeliever, between church and world, other than the distinction that the one does know, and the other does not know, its own misery. But it is evident that the Scriptures sound a different note about this distinction. The Bible, while fully maintaining the difference, demands meekness. This is evident in the peculiar use of the pronoun "we," which recurs in Scripture. The history of Nehemiah, for instance, speaks with undeniable discriminating force against the opponents of the work of God: "The God of heaven, he will prosper us; therefore we his servants will arise and build: but ye have no portion, nor right, nor memorial, in Jerusalem" (Neb. 2:20). Lest we should imagine that only the fervor of Nehemiah could produce such language, let us turn to the New Testament. There the "we" is also stressed: "But we are not of them that shrink back unto perdition; but of them that have faith unto the saving of the soul" (Heb. 10:39).

A superficial consideration of these words would suggest that we have here the limit of self-elevation, a spirit showing all the symptoms of a separation invented to suit one's own convenience. A closer scrutiny reveals that the distinction is possible and meaningful, and does not conflict with the message of grace. This is indeed the narrow way, skirted on both sides by treacherous ravines. To be able to walk on this road is the work and miracle of the Holy Spirit. Everything depends on whether this "we" magnifies the grace of God or whether the grace of God is understood as a pedestal on which to elevate the "we." Thus election and grace may be dangerously misconceived; and the self-deluded are bound to get mired in a private cultus, whether moral or religious, instead of being driven out to glorify God and to serve their neighbor. At this point the message of grace is made servicable to a horrific self-glorification which is all the more dangerous because it recognizes the grace of God. To such cultists the Word of God in Amos is no longer intelligible: "You only have I known of all the families of the earth: therefore will I visit upon you all your iniquities" (Amos 3:2).

Under these circumstances, the grace of God, instead of being central in our lives, becomes a phase of the past, and the "we" a flight from it. The self-assertion that remains now negates the salvation that is from above.

Those, however, who would preclude self-praise by condemning all activity and commending passivity, are equally in error. They remind us of the man in the parable who buried his talent and who thought that by not doing anything he could escape all the dangers attending the coming of his "hard" master (Matt. 25:24). The real problem of self-praise is set in the midst of activity, in the midst of following after holiness. This activity is particularly patent in the words of Paul: "Work out your own salvation with fear and trembling, for it is God who worketh in you both to will and to do for his good pleasure." In his commentary on Philippians, Barth places all the emphasis on "fear and trembling" but he does not deny that the believer is viewed here as a living, active organism.[4] Paul's assertion is the more striking because, rather than contrasting God's work with man's work, he cites the work of God as an incentive for the work of man. God's work in salvation, in Paul's view, never absorbs or invalidates man's work, but arouses and stimulates it and gives it meaning.

The relation between the two workings cannot be described in the words of Barth: "Our faith that is never under any circumstances we ourselves," or in terms of what he says on Chapter 3, verse 12: "My being appropriated by Christ needs no correlative on my part; it cannot even have it," or in terms of his view on faith, which is not, he says, "the act of human belief, but the act of the original divine belief."[5]

Although Barth has later corrected some of these extreme pronouncements, it is clear what he meant to say. He wishes to avoid lapsing into independent human activity. He is afraid of a subjective pole of correlativity opposite to an objective pole, and tries to find a solution by introducing a divine subjectivity. But free and sovereign grace does not abolish human subjectivity. Paul wants to bring out that in this actual correlativity the grace of God must be honored. There lies the mystery of the gift of the Spirit. Amid the full reality of daily life, amid the activities of human faith, the judgment of God falls upon all self-praise. The focal point in all striving is always the grace of God: its comforts and its

---

4. Karl Barth, *Philipperbrief*, page 42.
5. *Ibid.*, page 98.

warnings. Hence Jerusalem is searched with lanterns. Jerusalem must be shaken out of its false self-admiration: "Gather yourselves together, yes, gather together, O nation that hath no shame . . . . Seek ye Jehovah, all ye meek of the earth, that have kept his ordinances; seek righteousness, seek meekness: it may be ye will be hid in the day of Jehovah's anger" (Zeph. 2:1, 3). From pride they are called to meekness and from shamelessness to seeking righteousness — that is the grace which calls them out of pseudo-isolation and fancied independence. Man must learn what is good for him: "It is a good thing to give thanks unto Jehovah. And to sing praises unto thy name, O most High" (Psalm 92:1).

Clearly, the grace of God and praises sung to his name must be dominant in the correlation between faith and sanctification. The connection between sanctification and meekness is visible as well. At this point looms a problem. For if sanctification is what the Bible says it is, is not a sense of self, and the danger of viewing sanctification as an achievement of our own, inevitable? This danger did not seem acute in connection with justification, for there the ungodly are the object of divine grace. But in sanctification, can we still speak of "sola-gratia"? Are we not certain, on the way of progressive sanctification, to sense the value of our effort, our struggle, our conquests? Is it possible that we, by our opposition, put the devil to flight and fail to sense a connection between our opposition and his flight?

Do we not in some small measure transcend meekness in our sanctification?

We recall with what clarity the Scriptures speak about glorying. Paul distinguished true from false glorying when he said: "He that glorieth, let him glory in the Lord." This glorying is expressed in many ways. God has elected to shame the strong and the wise; he has chosen the base things of the world, and the things that are despised, and the things that are not, that he might bring to nought the things that are: that no flesh should glory before God (I Cor. 1:27-29). To the church he says: "For who makest thee to differ? and what hast thou that thou didst not receive? but if thou didst receive it, why dost thou glory as if thou hadst not received it?" (I Cor. 4:7). False glorying is reprehensible. As for Paul he glories in the hope of the glory of God and in tribulations (Rom. 5:2). True glorying is an echo of sovereign grace. Every other kind of glorying, because it wells up from a feeling of self-sufficiency, is damnable in the sight of God. This sin of false glorying is always leering from a corner.

There is a crudely candid glorying such as that of Edom who, deceived by the pride of his heart, boasted: "Who shall bring me down to the ground?" (Obadiah 3, 4), and that of Nineveh, the city that dwelt carelessly, which said: "I am, and there is none besides me" (Zeph. 2:15). But there is also a more concealed glorying which does not deny the grace of God. It is the glorying of the grateful Pharisee; it is that of everyone who begins his course acknowledging the unmerited grace of God and pursues it by relying on his own merits. In this manner fellowship with God is broken. Over against all public and private self-praise is the message that God, exclusively, is the praise of Israel (Deut. 10:21). This praise is accompanied by jubilation and joy. Where then is the glorying? Paul asks. It is excluded. By what manner of law? By the law of faith! (Rom. 3:27). Sola-fide banishes all self-praise, not only in the beginning but throughout the life of sanctification. The phrase, "without the works of the law," is identical in meaning with glorying in God, in the Cross, in the gift of God. There is no difference between earlier and later stages. Graphically Paul warns against the gentile Christians who, freshly grafted in the trunk of Israel, were inclined to feel superior to the Jews: "But if some of the branches were broken off, and thou, being a wild olive, wast grafted in among them, and didst become a partaker with them of the root of the fatness of the olive tree; glory not over the branches: but if thou gloriest it is not thou that bearest the root, but the root thee . . . . Be not highminded, but fear" (Rom. 11:17-20). This is the faith in which they must stand, having been grafted in by grace. Self-glorification is possible only through unbelief, which may move God, who spared not the natural branches, to remove also the highminded gentile Christian.

Thus the Scriptures preach humility: the only suitable response to the mercy of God. This humility is not to be sloughed off as believers advance to new levels but to be preserved as long as grace communicates itself.

It has been asserted that this teaching is at times contradicted in Scripture. In certain of the Psalms a sense of self-esteem seems to rise to the surface, most conspicuously in Psalm 26, where the writer speaks of himself in terms almost indistinguishable from those used by the Pharisees. "Judge me, O Jehovah, for I have walked in mine integrity." ". . . I have walked in thy truth. I have not sat with men of falsehood; neither will I go in with dissemblers. I hate the assembly of evildoers, and will not sit with the wicked. I will wash my hands in innocency" (Psalm 26:1, 3). Is there not a striking similarity here with the words used by the Pharisee in the parable?

Let no one jump to conclusions. There is in this psalm a definite center to which all these utterances are related. The poet trusts in the Lord, whose lovingkindness is before his eyes. In God's truth he has walked. He compasses the altar of Jehovah and loves the habitation of Jehovah's house. He makes the voice of thanksgiving to be heard and tells of all God's wondrous works. And finally: In the congregation will I bless Jehovah.

Each of these statements undercuts Pharisaism. The expression of joy over the mercy of God and distinguishing self from others are naturally related; they find their point of convergence on the altar of reconciliation.

In what does this integrity consist? — asks Valeton. And he answers: "In that the poet trusts, unwaveringly, and always, in Jehovah; from a Christian point of view, we would say, in that he *believes*. These two thoughts are pregnant and give birth to the genuinely Israelitish, Pauline idea of justification by faith." It is impossible, as Eduard Köning does, to view Psalm 26 as an echo of Pharisaic self-righteousness. The poet, he says, does not bring out the priority of divine grace and fails to understand that at best we are still unprofitable servants of God — without merit of our own. People who talk like the psalmist are the healthy people who need no physician.

In this manner an injustice is done to what Psalm 26 says about the mercy of God, about his altar and habitation. The whole is a song of praise. It is possible, of course, for a Pharisee to absorb the mercy of God and the altar into his own nomistic scheme; but it is also possible that in the psalms the voice of a believer speaks of the righteousness which is not subversive of the grace of God. There seems to be a contradiction between knowing that one walks in faith on the paths of righteousness and trusting in the mercy of God alone. The Psalmist abhors the workers of iniquity and claims at the same time that he trusts in Jehovah (Ps. 28:3-5, 7); he hates them that regard lying vanities and prays for God's mercy (Ps. 31:6, 9); and so it is possible for God to love the righteous (Ps. 146:8).

Whoever gives an abstract moral interpretation to these Old-Testament expressions of righteousness is bound to distort the Scriptures. He would make of Israel's religion and the Covenant of Grace a purely nomistic salvation. The holiness of the righteous could then be only an ethical ideal and the mercy of God becomes irrelevant.

"Who shall dwell in thy holy hill? He that walketh uprightly, and worketh righteousness, and speaketh truth in his heart" (Ps. 15:1). Has morality become — this may be our question — the basis for religion? sincerity and righteousness the ground for dwelling on the holy hill? Or have we here an expression of a people which kisses the scepter of grace extended to it from the sanctuary? Psalm 24 gives the answer. First it repeats the sentiment of Psalm 15: "Who shall ascend into the hill of Jehovah? ... He that hath clean hands and a pure heart; who hath not lifted up his soul unto falsehood, and hath not sworn deceitfully." But then it adds: "He shall receive a blessing from Jehovah, and righteousness from the God *of his salvation.*" Nothing here smacks of a moral relationship. "This is the generation of them that seek after him, that seek thy face ..." (verse 6). The righteousness of the Psalms, unlike the righteousness that vaunts itself and thrives on personal merit, is in strict accord with the demand of Paul: "He that glorieth, let him glory in the Lord."

Another question is whether, besides a faith in God, we cannot also speak of a faith in man. The problem was broached by Heering who complained about the "defective anthropology of the Reformers." He acknowledges the correctness of their self-evaluation but cannot see that this should be applied to one's neighbor. A withering self-criticism is fine: not its extension to others. The acknowledgement of one's own impotence is appropriate: not the assumption of another's.

It is evident that this view is untenable. The Reformers did not teach a religious disqualification on the basis of subjective experience, but they expressed the guilt which, according to Scripture, rests upon all. God's Revelation teaches a "general" disqualification of man; the mind of the flesh, it says, is enmity against God, so that not so much as one is good. This is the general, but very concrete, expression of the holy wrath of God (Compare Romans I).

Heering has run aground on a double evalutation of man. Religious self-disqualification issues either from an underestimate of man's capacities or from the Revelation of God. Humility, based on a hypertrophied sense of sin, rests on a fiction; humility, induced by an encounter with the truth, is organic with genuine sanctification. Hence we reject Heering's solution. The only remaining possibility is that confession of sin is a genuine confession of genuine sin.

Confession, according to the Scriptures, embraces both the past and the present. Owing to the miracle of his forgiveness, God says he will no more remember the sins of his people (Isaiah 43:25), he treads them under foot and casts them into the depths of the sea (Micah 7:19). It is the glory of forgiveness that God averts his mind and eye from our iniquity. But God's act of not remembering our sins does not correspond with our "forgetting." Forgiveness corresponds rather with confession of guilt, gratitude for forgiveness, and humble reminiscence. This remembering is part of gratitude. Paul, for instance, reflected often on past sins. He tasted the mercy of God and now sees the greatness of that mercy against the background of his guilt. He calls himself the chief of sinners and the least of the apostles, not even worthy of being called an apostle because he had persecuted the church. Forgiveness does not erase all memory of guilt but stands out in striking relief because of it; and the guilt is the blacker for the mercy that removed it. For Paul to call himself the least of all the saints is to magnify the grace of God which gave him the unspeakable riches of preaching Christ. The humility of believers is not merely related to the past, however; it also concerns present guilt. For the present they ask: "Forgive us this day our trespasses." In the present the sinfulness of their lives is exposed in the light of Christ's presence: "Depart from me, for I am a sinful man, O Lord" (Luke 5:8). The believing centurion cries out: "Lord, trouble not thyself; for I am not worthy that thou shouldest come under my roof. . ." (Luke 7:6). His reputation, however, was that "he is worthy that thou shouldest do this for him; for he loveth our nation, and himself built us our synagogue" (Luke 7:4, 5). And Jesus says of him: "I say unto you, I have not found so great faith, no, not in Israel" (Luke 7:9).

This sense of unworthiness is genuine; it does not spring from a religious undervaluation of self but from a humility induced by divine grace. It is the humility of the returning prodigal: "I am not worthy to be called thy son." One is struck everywhere by the powerful sense of present unworthiness. Truly these men, who would glory, gloried in the Lord.

A sense of guilt is not gradually pushed back by a sense of holiness. Indeed, if sanctification were a process of "improvement," a sense of guilt would gradually evaporate. But sanctification as increased immersion in the grace and knowledge of Jesus Christ must result in a deeper sense of unworthiness. Of course, this perspective is thinkable only when sanctification remains tethered to faith.

The error of making sanctification a moralistic process is, according to Kuyper, at the bottom of Catholicism as well as Modernism. Rome "did violence to the holiness of God to the extent that it presented holiness to man as something attainable to him, as something he might by fierce effort approach and at length acquire."[6] But this mode of thinking is bound to produce an insidious self-esteem. It is surely not the holiness of the branches that abide in the vine and so produce much fruit.

The idea that sanctification follows justification is, at bottom, a violation of the grace of God: for it posits a substitute for the grace of God or tries to complete it with human works. Never, according to Barth, can the believer claim his good works as his own possession and contrast them with the non-

---

6. Abraham Kuyper, *Uit het Woord,* first series I, page 226.

possession of another man.[7] In true holiness it is not hard to understand that our works cannot even be a part of our righteousness since they are polluted and imperfect. When the Catechism speaks of the imperfection of our good works, it intends to express our guilt; it complains humbly in the obedience of faith that we are still so far removed not from some moral ideal but from the Lord. At this point sanctification and humility come together. Paul's "pressing on," in Philippians 3, is certainly not aimed at moral improvement; his aim is to gain Christ (Phil. 3:8). This pursuit is in utter contrast with self-righteousness. In this pursuit Paul can forget what is behind and press on to what is ahead. All is motion here and sweeping activity, activity founded on the high calling of God in Christ Jesus.

No one understood Paul better than John Calvin who wrote: "We are not our own; therefore let us, as far as possible, forget ourselves and all things that are ours. On the contrary, we are God's; to him, therefore, let us live and die. We are God's; therefore let his wisdom and will preside in all our actions. We are God's; towards him, therefore, as our only legitimate end, let every part of our lives be directed. O, how great a proficiency has that man made, who, having been taught that he is not his own, has taken the sovereignty and government of himself from his own reason, to surrender it to God!"[8] This activity is steeped in humility. For this reason, Calvin could say: "Christ therefore justifies no one whom he does not also sanctify."[9]

When David prayed that the Lord should not enter into judgment with his servant, he was speaking, says Calvin, "en sa plus grande perfection." This expression makes sense only if sanctification is understood also as mortification and self-

---

7. Karl Barth, *Römerbrief*, page 204.
8. John Calvin, *Institutes*, III, VII, 1.
9. *Ibid.*, III, XVI, 1.

denial. But to travel this road is to enter into a fuller light
— a light in which believers have fellowship with each other
and their Redeemer.

Thus the believer proceeds from strength to strength. "O
Jehovah of hosts, blessed is the man that trusteth in thee"
(Ps. 84:7, 12).

The Imitation of Christ

CHAPTER VII

The Imitation of Christ

IT IS impossible to write about sanctification in terms of Holy Writ without taking account of the imitation of Christ. For the entire life of believers, enveloped as it is by the demands of sanctification, can be epitomized as imitation: imitation in the sense of following in the steps of Another. The imitation of Christ is not merely a form of sanctification, one among several, but a description of its essence.

The history of the church being replete with distortions of and controversy concerning the imitation of Christ, the problem merits our unstinted attention. The "Imitation of Christ," written by Thomas a Kempis, aroused a great deal of reaction; and in this reaction one may perceive how reluctant people were to describe the life of sanctification in terms of imitation. The charge was that to imitate, or copy, the deeds which Christ performed on earth was to force the Christian life into a new moralistic strait jacket. Worse, such imitation was at least a partial denial of the unique significance of the Mediatorial work of Jesus Christ, who alone had stood before the Father, on behalf of the lost, as Messiah and High Priest. Christ as Mediator versus Christ as Example — that was the contrast. Instead of imitation there should be faith in Christ's redeeming life and sacrificial death.

Since the significance of Christ as example is certainly in need of careful definition, this reaction to "copying" him is natural. The imitation of Christ was in fact thought to consist in many varying forms.

135

Some contended for imitation of Christ's suffering and crossbearing, in humility, gentleness, or voluntary poverty. In periods of great worldliness, preachers of repentance would travel through the land proclaiming that the strangle hold of the world could be shaken off only by a return to the simplicity of the life of Christ. St. Francis of Assisi especially was a popular model of poverty and unworldliness. Imitation of Christ was associated particularly with certain classes of people, martyrs, monks, and ascetics. The idea was the attainment of conformity with Christ — a conformity evident, for instance, in the stigmata which St. Francis bore. Some championed the imitation of the virtues of Christ, others the imitation of his actions. Men were called upon utterly to forsake the world and to dwell in the atmosphere of the holy life of Christ in order to body forth its purity and unflagging dedication.

This is not to say that these theories concerning the imitation of Christ allow no room for the aspect of redemption. The Middle Ages still sensed too strongly the uniqueness of Christ, his life and death — of which the eucharist was a continual reminder — to reduce the imitation of Christ merely to a painful pursuit of an ethical ideal. Even in the work of Thomas a Kempis there are occasional flashes of the incomparable power of grace in the sacrifice of Christ. He does draw a parallel between the sacrifice of Christ and our sacrifice but in his exposition of the first there is decided evidence of its atoning nature: "Lord, I offer unto Thee, on Thy propitiatory altar, all my sins and offences, which I have committed before Thee and Thy Holy Angels, from the day wherein I first could sin even to this hour; that Thou mayest consume and burn them, one and all, with the fire of Thy love, and blot out all the stains of my sins, and cleanse my conscience from every offence, and restore to me Thy grace which by sinning I lost, fully forgiving me all, and admitting me mercifully to the kiss of peace."[1]

Although the atonement is nowhere openly controverted in this book, mention of it is spasmodic and eclipsed by "imitation." None of the fundamental truths of Christianity is, in fact, explicitly denied in the "Imitatio Christi." The problem we actually confront in this connection is how to relate the ideas operative in imitation to the Gospel of reconciliation.

Important in the history of the "imitation" of Christ is the role played by the heavily stressed human nature of our Lord. His life was claimed to be the absolute norm for all Christian living. This idea has again received emphasis in current Catholic ethics. Ethics itself was defined as "the scientific exposition of the imitation of Christ in private as well as communal life." Whereas in Roman ethics there is a distinction between natural and supernatural virtues, the supernatural virtues were said to be infused by Christ and embodied by him in normative living. Christ's life, his suffering, and his death, were all part of one great example; this example is normative without, of course, being a model to be minutely copied. Catholic theology often asserts — rather simplistically — that the sacrificial death of Christ does not put a fence around his life: its value for all who would see God lies in the pattern and program embodied in it. The saints have all lived with but one ideal: To reproduce that pattern in their own lives. Daily they renewed their efforts to become little "Christs." That, they said, is the only way to avert the disasters piling up on this world's horizon. That, too, is the inexorable demand of Christ. The alternative is annihilation. Our lives must be transformed after the example and doctrine of Christ; following in his steps we shall join him in conquering and redeeming the world.

---

1. Thomas à Kempis. *The Imitation of Christ.* Book IV, Chapter IX.

Noteworthy in this peroration is the conclusion that we share in the conquest and redemption of the world. It is quite clear in this idiom of activism how inadequate is the disavowal of "copying" Christ. Even with this restriction the Gospel may recede into a moralistic haze — a danger for which the very word "imitatio" is largely to blame.[2]

The countless distortions of the imitation of Christ may not, however, lead us to discredit its significance. Though opposed to all moralism, Kuyper warned: "The life of the church would be needlessly impoverished if, from an aversion to frequent abuse, it should neglect the precious truth offered to the believer in the imitation of Christ."[3] Everything depends on getting the imitation in true Scriptural perspective.

Time and again the Bible records that Christ appealed to others to follow him. Following Jesus is shown to be a decisive occurrence. "I am the light of the world: he that followeth me shall not walk in the darkness, but shall have the light of life" (John 8:12). Sometimes Jesus is general in his appeal, and at other times, very specific. To Simon and Andrew plying their nets and to Levi sitting in the place of toll comes the magnetic call "Follow thou me." The wondrous light of the future already falls upon those who follow Christ: "Verily I say unto you, that ye who have followed me, in the regeneration when the Son of man shall sit on the throne of his glory, ye also shall sit upon twelve thrones, judging the twelve tribes of Israel" (Matt. 19:28). Overpowering blessings accrue to the followers of Christ but also great sacrifices are demanded: houses, brothers, sisters, father, mother, and children. Theirs, after all, is the inheritance of eternal life (Matt. 19:29). Christ himself does not cease to make clear the seriousness of the decision to follow him. The scribe who contemplated discipleship is told to weigh his decision. For

2. Influential, also, was Augustine's dictum: "Quid est enim sequi nisi imitari?" (For what does it mean "to follow" if not "to imitate"?)
3. Abraham Kuyper, *Uit het Woord*, first series 1, page 475.

"foxes have holes, and the birds of the heaven have nests; but the Son of man hath not where to lay his head" (Matt. 8:19, 20). And he that does not take his cross and follow after him, is not worthy of him (Matt. 10:38).

No elaborate explanation is required to show that these expressions indicate not a bare imitation of Christ but a going and remaining with him, choosing for him and continuing to choose for him, receiving him amid the crisis that is being consummated between him and Israel. With Christ the Kingdom has come: the hour of decision has arrived. The Christ is set for the falling and rising of many in Israel (Luke 2:34); blessed is he, whosoever shall find no occasion of stumbling in him (Matt. 11:6). The call comes to the people to receive the message of redemption — after serious consideration, that is — to follow him wherever he goes, and to listen to whatever he says. "My sheep hear my voice, and I know them, and they shall never perish" (John 10:27). To follow the Christ in this fashion evinces total surrender. His voice penetrates into all the nooks and crannies of the soul; loyalty to him overrules all other loyalties. The normal relationships and obligations of life are rehabilitated and made relative to the Kingdom and to the Kingship of Christ. At the center is the Kingdom and all wills and wishes must be bent in its direction. Self-denial is not negative: it is positive re-direction of the total being.

The call to follow Christ is all-inclusive. The followers of Christ must have no reluctances and reservations; they must abide with him and thus share in his salvation, dwell in his light. profess his truth, and draw on his life. Though the threat of opposition and even of violent death may cast its shadow upon such crossbearing, the faithful know that no one will snatch them out of the hand of the Master.

The significance of these words reaches out far beyond the times in which they were spoken. Without underestimating the special bond existing between Jesus and his disciples, we must be prepared to hear these words echoing and re-echoing through the church of the ages. Their universality was already evident when Jesus spoke them; purposely and explicitly Jesus took into the sphere of his teaching and praying those who would believe in him through the words of the apostles (John 17:20). Of the 144,000 it is said (Rev. 14:4): "These are they that follow the Lamb whithersoever he goeth," words descriptive only of the radically committed: they let him, the Lamb, determine directions.

In this respect, too, the New Testament reiterates and reinterprets the Old Testament. The people of Israel were continually told to follow Jehovah. Elijah throws in the teeth of the people this option: Follow Jehovah or follow Baal. God's anger is ignited against those who had not wholly followed him (Numbers 32:11, 12) and precipitates a punishment lasting forty years. Not to follow Jehovah is to reject him and to go whoring after other gods. What this following implies is clearly stated: "You shall walk after Jehovah your God, and fear him, and keep his commandments, and obey his voice, and ye shall serve him, and cleave unto him" (Deut. 13:4).

When the people wander away from the Lord they must repent, return, and follow him anew. Following God is the fulfilment of the first commandment. The people must incline their hearts to Jehovah and so serve him and listen to his voice (Joshua 24:23, 24).

Those who return to Jehovah shall dwell under his shadow and blossom as the vine. "Ephraim shall say, What have I to do anymore with idols? . . . Who is wise, that he may understand these things? prudent, that he may know them? for the ways of Jehovah are right, and the just shall walk in them; but transgressors shall fall therein" (Hosea 14:8-10).

This call to follow Jehovah is clearly the same as the call to follow Jesus Christ. Their content is identical. The voice that spoke from heaven on the mount of Transfiguration can, as well as the appeals of Deuteronomy, be taken as a call to follow the Christ: "This is my beloved Son: hear ye him" (Mark 9:7). To "hear" the Christ is to follow him in intimate fellowship.

This is not to say, however, that we have now exhausted the meaning of the Scriptural injunction to follow the Lord. With respect to the preceding givens it would be hard to speak of the "imitation" of Christ. And the imitation of Christ does not consist in walking on the trails he has blazed but in a particular way of walking with and after him. To follow someone may mean to march under his command, to be under his direction, and to serve him in utter obedience. But there are many passages in the New Testament which indicate a more specific manner in which to follow the Christ, that is, to follow him as an example.

First let us turn to Peter. He is busily exhorting his readers when, with an abrupt shift, he turns their attention to Christ. He has just admonished household servants to submit to their masters, not only to the good and gentle but also to the difficult (I Peter 2:18). Quite contrary to human instincts, he declares that it is grace if a man suffers injustice and endures grief for God's sake. There is no value, he says, in getting punished when one has generously deserved it but if a man gets reprimanded or buffeted for doing his duty and bears it patiently he may rejoice in the grace of God. Then of a sudden, against this background of servants and masters, of doing good and receiving evil, there rises the profile of the Man of Sorrows in whose life particularly the combination of innocence and suffering was illustrated. He did no sin, neither was guile found in his mouth (I Peter 2:22). And his suffering did not produce rebellion or retribution; when he was insulted he offered no insult in return and when he suffered he uttered no threats.

Into a tired old world, where accounts must always be settled and old scores paid off, entered at long last One who did not demand blood for blood. Peter is fascinated afresh by the mystery of the suffering Christ; as well as by the awesome silence of Golgotha which tore this system of revenge and counter-revenge, of rebellion and counter-rebellion, from its creaking hinges. And the man on the street, the everyday sort of believer, says Peter, must somehow link his life to the mystery of this suffering. He must take the blows patiently and not in a mood of drab resignation or powerless resentment. "For hereunto were ye called: because Christ also suffered for you, leaving you an example, that ye should follow his steps" (I Peter 2:21).

In any attempt to understand the imitation of Christ, this passage of Peter should be decisive. For there is here no general instruction to walk in the steps of the Master but a specific directive to imitate him in his suffering. Again, to imitate him in this respect does not mean to copy or reproduce his suffering. Peter does not provide a model to be punctiliously reproduced; he points out rather that Christ has suffered for us (I Peter 2:21) and that he bore our sins in his body upon the tree, "that we, having died unto sins, might live unto righteousness; by whose stripes ye were healed" (I Peter 2:24). Hence those who follow do not have to repeat anything: they are healed. Their suffering never runs parallel to, is never a reproduction of, his sufferings; the redemptive suffering of Christ is final and controls every admonition in Peter's epistle. The call to be imitators comes to those who were going astray like sheep, but are now returned unto the Shepherd of their souls (verse 25). The Example is at the same time Shepherd in the full sense of the word.

Following in the steps of the Shepherd: that is the kind of conformity propagated by Peter. This is the kind of conformity which excludes mere imitation. It is a conformity related to Christ's act of abolishing sin. At bottom, it is to live conformably to, and on the basis of, the Atonement. On this basis alone believers are called to walk in his steps. They are now sheep of his flock. And they are to walk not on paths that will at length lead to communion with Christ but on the path that lies open because of the communion with Christ which they enjoy right along. In being united with him they will, in all their suffering, show forth the grace which they possess in virtue of communion with him. Their communion in faith becomes manifest and the reactions natural to this world are subdued: revenge, insult and threats.

They have communion with the suffering of Christ. By the Atonement he cleared the title deed on them and now they are his. Believers no longer have the right to dispose of their lives as they see fit. Hence they take up the cross of self-denial and join the Man of Sorrows. As partakers of grace they yield to death their old lives — vast complexes of sinful reactions — and make also their suffering conformable to the example of Christ. For to be a cross-bearer is to have surrendered all authority to Christ. The life of the cross-bearer is not one of austere imitation but rather one of conformity rooted in reconciliation.

In the same way Paul abruptly breaks off his exhortation to call attention to Jesus Christ (Phil. 2:5-8) and his humiliation.

He had admonished the Philippians to be of one mind, to do their duty in lowliness of mind, to look to the things of others, and now he continues: "Have this mind in you which was also in Christ Jesus." To illustrate this "mind" of Christ he points out how Christ emptied himself and was obedient even to the death of the Cross. Paul does not explicitly, as Peter, mention that Christ's self-humiliation was subservient to the Atonement but there is actually no difference between them. Paul is as little interested as Peter in some incidental example or a relatively abstract obedience to given orders, but he urges conformity to the mind of Christ as it appeared in his self-humiliation. Paul does not ask that the Philippians copy the life of Christ but that they know themselves as called to be like-minded.

Repeatedly in the New Testament this association of ideas comes up. Paul says in the epistle to the Romans that we must not please ourselves but our neighbor that he may be built up, "for Christ also pleased not himself"˙ (Rom. 15:3). There is a connection, says Paul, between the generosity of the churches in Macedonia and the grace of Christ who, though he was rich, became poor for our sakes, that we through his poverty might become rich (II Cor. 8:9). Let there be tolerance and forgiveness, says Paul, if any man have a complaint: "Even as the Lord forgave you, so also do ye (Col. 3:13) and walk in love "even as Christ also loved you" (Eph. 5:2). The result will be that peace will rule in the hearts of believers (Col. 3:15) and they will be thankful in truly bearing love to one another which is the bond of perfection. Conformity to Christ is the substance of gratitude. Three times Paul underlines gratitude in this passage (Col. 3:15-17). The Bible even speaks of imitating God: "Be ye therefore imitators of God as beloved children" (Eph. 5:1). This combination is explained by the preceding: "Be ye kind one to another, tenderhearted, forgiving each other, even as God also in Christ forgave you" (Eph. 4:32). Here also we perceive that the imitation of Christ and the imitation of God are most intimately related to God's act of forgiving love in Christ: "God was in Christ reconciling the world unto himself" (II Cor. 5:19). All legalism is taboo: "Be ye therefore imitators of God as beloved children; and walk in love even as Christ also loved you and gave himself up for us" (Eph. 5:1, 2).

Occasionally, from a reaction to unsound imitation, there have been voices in favor of substituting the notion of obedience. It is clear, however, that the imitation of Christ rightly conceived can never conflict with obedience. One is bound to impoverish the New Testament revelation if he speaks so

emphatically about obedience as to neglect the idea of imitation. Fear of imitation was nearly always motivated by a
justified fear of moralism. But no one should forget that also
by neglecting the Scriptural teaching of imitation a man may
lapse into moralism. Those who shy away from imitation
sometimes speak of "marching under his command" — as
if that phrase is proof against legalistic corruption. In any
event, the relationship between the Master and his imitators
is one of faith and any obedience whatever is conditioned by
that relationship. We conclude that both to stress the imitation and to neglect it may lead to a new moralism which
though it does not deny the atonement tends to crowd it out
with a legalistic conception of obedience. Only a sound interpretation of the imitation of Christ, an interpretation which
proceeds from his redeeming grace, can protect the church
from this fatal declension.

In order to describe the imitation of Christ, people have
frequently employed the distinction between "internal" and
"external" imitation. Over against those who wished to imitate various deeds of Christ — to the extent of toting a
wooden cross — there were those who stressed the imitation
of his inner life, his love, patience, tolerance, and obedience.
They realized that the imitation of his deeds was in conflict
with his unique Person and exclusive mediatorial work. And
so, as does the classic work of Thomas a Kempis, they laid
all stress on the inner life of Christ.

Bringing out the importance of this internal imitation has
often been credited to Luther. He did not favor the ascetic
life, did full justice to common, everyday life with its God-
given ordinances, and rejected an austere imitation of given
aspects of Jesus' life. According to Seeberg the imitation of
Christ consists in this: "The follower of the example of Christ
is he who, like Christ, devotes his entire life with all his talents
and powers simply, quietly, and unreservedly, to the service
of God, be he man or woman, married or unmarried, rich or

poor, in a humble or in a high position, weak or strong, solitary or a member of a large organization." From this we may conclude that we should imitate not the deeds but the dedicated life of Christ. Against the external imitation of Christ there has been ceaseless opposition. It was simply impossible to copy the deeds of Christ, to reproduce his actions in the temple or his words as spoken to Herod and Pilate, or to duplicate his poverty and celibacy. Calvin mentions Christ's walking on the sea, his cleansing a leper, his raising the dead, his fasting for forty days, and says that these acts had a different purpose from that of being copied. Hence many people had recourse to another imitation. The inner brilliance of his ineffable virtues radiating outward through his actions — that would be, they thought, our God-given example. Not his actions which were, after all, integral with his work as Mediator and adapted to his own times, but his inner attitudes, devotion to the Father, and holy purpose in all his striving, are illustrative of what God, the Holy One, demands of us in his law.

In this manner the idea of imitation in the sense of copying, though limited to the inner life of Christ, remains in force. The imitation of Christ in this sense becomes in fact a strenuous striving after a distant ideal — becoming like the Holy One. The inner life of Jesus is said to illustrate the law of God — a law valid also for us — and his fulfilment of the law becomes an example to be followed. Thus the law embodied in the attitudes of Christ became a new law and hence a new temptation. It is not surprising, therefore, that this inner imitation, no less than the external, produced so much anxiety and uncertainty and so little joy. This yoke was anything but easy. The imitation of Christ tends thus to harden into a moral ideal to be virtuously pursued; from this ideal to a refined self-torture and thence to the struggle for perfection is only a small step. What this implies can be clearly seen in the lives of certain people unfortunate enough to be canonized;

it ends in self-torment and solitary meditation — the righteousness of good works. How remote this is from the comfort and clarity of Peter's words: "By whose stripes ye were healed." And how great the contrast between these solitary imitators delighting in their joylessness and the believers who, walking in the light of true imitation, delight in the communion of saints and exercise forgiveness and patience.

The New Testament breaks with this imitation, be it external or internal; instead of pushing the believer into a heavy harness of moral attainment it places him in sweet communion with the Master. This communion is the same for his disciples after the Ascension as it was before. For the imitation to which he called them during his sojourn on earth is possible only through faith and by his grace. The possibility of coming to him and walking with him is always owing to the initiative of divine grace: "No man can come to me, except the Father that sent me draw him: and I will raise him up in the last day" (John 6:44).

It is phenomenal that Jesus, a few moments before his earthly career came to an end, should provide a moving illustration of the imitation he requires — namely, in washing the feet of his disciples (John 13). In this dramatic event a merely literal imitation is excluded, nor is there any proclamation of moral ideals.

Now is the hour come!

Christ is about to depart to his Father above and, knowing that his hour was come, he loved his own that were in the world to the uttermost. The tension increases: the devil begins to manipulate the suggestible soul of Judas. And Jesus, knowing all this, arose, laid aside his garments, girded himself, and began to wash the feet of his disciples.

In response to Peter's refractoriness the Master reveals the gravity of the occasion: "If I wash thee not, thou hast no part with me." Hence this ablutionary drama is not simply a contribution to general philanthropy or an exhibition of humility but rather a sample of the Secret of Reconciliation.

His task accomplished, Jesus asks his disciples: "Know ye what I have done to you?" He, the Teacher and Lord, has washed their feet. "If I then, the Lord and the Teacher, have washed your feet, ye also ought to wash one another's feet. For I have given an example, that ye also should do as I have done to you" (John 13:14, 15). From this "as I have done to you," people have reasoned to a required copying of the act of Christ. But a careful scrutiny makes plain that in this example such imitation has no place. For all details have their climax in lustratory communion with the Master. If he does not wash their feet they have no part with him. And their washing each other's feet is to flow from his washing their feet. Here the imperative "ye ought" is based on the indicative "I have done." Because he has been merciful to them they owe it to each other likewise to be merciful. His love is to be the foundation of their lives and all their mutual relations. That little scene in the upper room is actually the epitome of his entire Mediatorial career; it symbolizes, in striking action, all the self-humiliation to which the Master put himself. And this self-humiliation of Christ must, for those who wish to follow him, become the rule. "A servant is not greater than his lord; neither one that is sent greater than he that sent him" (John 13:16). In this foot-washing incident it seemed indeed that the servants were greater than their lord. But exactly in token of his compassion and self-humiliation is Christ their Lord and causes them to share in his love.

This exhortation to follow Christ's example shows us that purification and reconciliation, so far from making the imitation of Christ less important, provide it with a rationale. The idea in true imitation is therefore to remember the mercies of Christ and thus "to have part" with him. Thus they will be servants of the Master and follow the Lamb "whithersoever he goeth."

The imitation of Christ cannot, therefore, be a prerogative of a special category of people: monks, martyrs, ascetics, or itinerant preachers. It is the privilege of every recipient of grace. By being made the possession of the Lord they are mercifully released from the illusion of isolation and autonomy and enlisted as his followers. Crucial in this imitation is the link between receiving mercy and being merciful, between forgiveness and readiness to forgive. It is therefore impossible to abstract the imitation of Christ from this example — embodying the unity of an act and a disposition to act — of voluntary self-humiliation. Kuyper grasped the core of it all when he wrote: "Whatever sidelights from the Scriptures one may bring to bear upon the imitation of Christ, they are all subsidiary to the one principal truth that he who could rightly claim all glory in heaven and on earth freely surrendered this glory in order, for our sake, to humble himself."[4]

Always, when the Scriptures exhort the believer to be as Christ, they point to the act of his love in the atonement for sin. This may seem strange since this act is his alone and we can and may recognize him as Mediator in this act alone, but the fact remains that the entire New Testament is in agreement on this point. This required conformity to an exclusive act of love would be a contradictory demand if it were a conformity to a law illustrated in the life of Christ: but it is possible nonetheless, and makes good sense, when it presupposes and flows from the Atonement.

Repeatedly the Bible presents this association of ideas. "A new commandment I give unto you, that ye love one another, even as I have loved you" (John 13:34). "If ye keep my commandments, ye shall abide in my love; even as I kept my Father's commandments, and abide in his love" (John

---

4. Abraham Kuyper, *Uit het Woord*, first series I, page 476.

15:10). This phrase "even as I" discloses a parallel and implies a conformity in which the sovereign love of God paves the way toward true imitation.

Throughout the New Testament, whenever the words "even as" are sounded whether in relation to God or to Christ, it is the mercy of God that receives all emphasis. The parable of the Unmerciful Servant ties in graphically with this theme. It is the story of a man up to his ears in debt who, though himself released from it, for some paltry shillings grabs another man by the throat. The cogency of the parable consists in the fact that this penny-snatching ingrate is delivered "to the tormentors, till he should pay all that was due" (Matt. 18:34). The consequence is inevitable: "So shall also my heavenly Father do unto you, if ye forgive not everyone his brother from your hearts" (Matt. 18:35). Although our deeds of mercy and forgiveness seem to precede the mercy of God, this parable makes plain both the priority of God's mercy and the obligations resulting from it.

This chain linking divine to human forgiveness, taught and explained as it is throughout the New Testament, points up the radical nature of the imitation of Christ. The imitation of Christ could never be part of the Good News, or the Evangel of Grace, were it a Via Dolorosa whose goal was God's grace; but because it receives its impetus from the revelation of God's antecedent grace, a grace unapplied for and unsolicited, therefore it is a wonderfully enriching evangelical truth. Not to heed it is a terrible denial of God's grace and so the concomitant threat is natural: "If ye forgive not, then. . . ." "Beloved, let us love one another: for love is of God; and everyone that loveth is begotten of God, and knoweth God" (I John 4:7).

The error of those who wished to create a sense of the urgent nature of the imitation of Christ was not that they passionately preached the need of repentance and revival; but that they so frequently muffed their assignment by pushing its compellingly evangelical aspect into the background. The plenitude of God's mercy was eclipsed by an imitation that consisted in laborious moral effort divorced from one's neighbor and inconsonant with the instruction of the entire New Testament. In response to all moralism it cannot be said too often that Christ spoke of a new law precisely with reference to his love (John 13:34). In connection with his love the newness of the commandment becomes intelligible. A perfunctory reading would suggest a contradiction in what John writes: "Beloved, no new commandment write I unto you, but an old commandment which ye had from the beginning: the old commandment is the word which ye heard. Again, a new commandment write I unto you, which thing is true in him and in you; because the darkness is passing away, and the true light already shineth" (I John 1:7, 8). But since he is writing about love to one's brother, the connection with John 13 is immediately apparent. Anyone inclined to infer from the "new commandment" of Christ that the Gospel has been vitiated by a legalistic spirit fails to understand the "newness" of the commandment. The newness of this commandment is not that *another* law has been set up for believers, for the commandment can be called both old and new without fear of inconsistency. But the old commandment is new since now, in the act of Christ's love, it has finally become fully and unmistakably manifest how truly this commandment also binds his followers in the communion of his love. The commandment is new partly because it is related to the new life generated by the Holy Spirit and partly because its fulfilment is the response of gratitude to the love of Christ. Gratitude being the fulfilment of this law, it can never impart to the imitation of Christ a tincture of legalism.

At times, with regard to the imitation of Christ, people have quoted a remarkable utterance of Paul: "Henceforth let no man trouble me; for I bear branded on my body the marks of Jesus" (Gal. 6:7). Paul here employs the word "stigma" and the question arises whether Paul forced his way through, even to the point of physical suffering, to the imitation of Christ in its extreme form.

Stigmatization arose in the thirteenth century, concurrently — and this is remarkable — with the florescence of the "imitatio Christi." The "imitatio" seemed to culminate, as it were, in the production of the stigmata of Christ: the divine seal upon long, lean years of arduous effort.

It was customary on the feast of the stigmatization of St. Francis to pray to Christ who, it was said, "renewed the holy stigmata of his suffering in the body of the blessed St. Francis, in order that the hearts of the believers might be kindled anew in love for the Crucified One."[5] According to Rome (several popes, such as Gregory IX and Alexander VI, spoke of the wonderful favor of God enjoyed by St. Francis) an act of God is crucial in stigmatization, but the upshot is nonetheless that "the problem of atonement occupies the foreground" and "the life of the 'stigmatized' is a chain of extraordinarily severe suffering in body and soul; it is the suffering of expiation."[6] It is evident that stigmatization interlocks with the "imitatio." This reproduction of the wounds of Christ's body, though not brought on by private effort, shows how far removed this imitation is from a concern for one's neighbor; how far removed it is also from what Paul meant with bearing the marks of Christ in his body. Frequently people did acknowledge that Paul was speaking about some other "stigmatization." Paul is obviously adverting to the scars and marks left by his work and by the maltreatment suffered in consequence of his communion with Christ. His are the scars of the missionary struggle. In harmony with the urgent admonitions of Peter, Paul saw "grace" in that suffering and in those marks, and in this happy frame of mind he followed in the steps of Christ.

---

5. *Wetzer und Welte's Kirchenlexikon, Stigmatisation,* XI, page 823.
6. *Ibid.,* page 824.

More important from the point of view of this chapter are those other words of Paul — favorite quoting material for Roman Catholic writers: "Now I rejoice in my sufferings for your sake, and fill up on my part that which is lacking of the afflictions of Christ in my flesh for his body's sake, which is the church" (Col. 1:24). Do we have a Scriptural basis after all for a synergistic co-suffering of the believer in imitation of Christ?

It is necessary for us to reflect on this "filling up that which is lacking," the more since the exegesis of Roman Catholics tends always to weaken the unique power of Christ's suffering and often places it squarely alongside of the suffering of believers. In his encyclical of 1943, Pope Pius XII said that, although our Savior has purchased by his suffering and death a limitless treasure of grace for his church, these gifts of grace are distributed gradually and their relative abundance depends largely on our good works, in virtue of which these divine gifts are freely bestowed upon the souls of men. In this manner, "we will, in the words of the Apostle, fill up in our flesh that which is lacking of the afflictions of Christ for his body's sake, which is the church." Not that Rome wishes to conclude from Col. 1:24 that the suffering of Christ is incomplete. Does not Pius XII speak of a limitless treasure of grace? But the trouble with the Reformation is, says Rome, that it does not tolerate any cooperation with the redemptive work of Christ whereas such cooperation is itself one of the glorious fruits of the redemption. According to Pius XII, believers need the help of a divine Redeemer but, however strange it may seem, Christ the Redeemer also needs the help of his members. In this connection, then, he speaks of "completion": "It is a comfort and joy to us Christians that our suffering has been raised to such a high plane in the Mystical Body of Christ that we can suffer and sacrifice with Christ for the communion of saints." The completion of Christ's suffering is organic with the entire scheme of Roman synergism and takes us into the same atmosphere as that of the Roman doctrine of the imitation of Christ.

Our problem is now whether this view of the "filling up on the suffering of Christ" is in accord with Holy Writ. At least this much is clear: Paul does not conceive of his sufferings as the buffetings of an imperious fate but rather as having meaning in relation to the church. It is suffering for Christ's sake and in virtue of his calling as minister of the Gospel. Paul too is a member of that communion of which Christ said to his disciples: "A servant is not greater than his lord. If they persecuted me, they will also persecute you" (John 15:20). In regard to this suffering Paul says that he fills up "that which is lacking of the afflictions of Christ." Owing to this "which-is-lacking" we are compelled to inquire whether perhaps Paul doubted the sufficiency of the suffering of Christ and must needs complete it. The idea of the insufficiency of the suffering of Christ, however, is completely foreign to Paul's way of thinking. Precisely as an antidote to the errors poisoning the church life at Colosse Paul had stressed the utter sufficiency of the suffering and death of Christ. The idea of completing the expiatory suffering of Christ was not Paul's but that of the false teachers! Because they have complicated the rich and simple truths of the Gospel, Paul has to point out the fullness of salvation in Christ Jesus (Col. 1:19, 20). Paul treats of the body of his flesh in which Christ through death has effected reconciliation (Col. 1:22). Christ has taken out of the way the bond written against us, nailing it to the cross (Col. 2:14), thus liquidating all our transgressions. For this reason, at any rate, it is clear that Paul does not mean that his suffering constitutes a part of the expiatory suffering of Christ.

There is, of course, a close tie between the suffering of Paul and that of Christ. Elsewhere he speaks of "the fellowship of his sufferings" (Phil. 3:10) and says that "the sufferings of Christ abound unto us" (I Cor. 1:5). But again, this fellowship in suffering does not complete the suffering and death of

Christ but flows from it: the sufferings which "abound unto us" are the ingredients of crossbearing in the steps of the Master, that is, crossbearing in the new situation created by the Atonement.

Therefore when Paul speaks of "filling up" what is lacking of the afflictions of Christ he means that his suffering constitutes a supplementary part of that total complex of suffering which issues from the cross of Christ. There is progress also in the suffering of Paul as a minister of the Gospel. He has labored more abundantly than any other apostles (I Cor. 15:10) and his suffering is proportionately severe. He is "always bearing about in the body the dying of Jesus" (II Cor. 4:10), an expression which is important also for Col. 1:24, particularly with a view to the succeeding: "For we who live are always delivered unto death for Jesus' sake, that the life also of Jesus may be manifested in our mortal flesh. So then death worketh in us, but life in you" (II Cor. 4:11, 12). On this most painful path Paul travels to make full the measure of suffering on behalf of the body of Christ. For this reason he rejoices in and about his sufferings. Such crossbearing in the steps of Christ is of great significance for the church of Christ.

From this center of communion with Christ the anodyne of comfort reaches out to the depths of their suffering. In the imitation of Christ the apostles, owing to their special mission, may be "a spectacle unto the world, both to angels and men," "men doomed to death," "the filth of world" (I Cor. 4:9, 13), but in their special crossbearing they never rise above the imitation of Christ taught as befitting the entire church throughout the New Testament. Amid all the suffering inflicted upon the apostles Paul can still say — an echo, as it were, of what Peter indicates as conformity to the Man of Sorrows: "Being reviled, we bless; being persecuted, we endure; being defamed, we entreat" (I Cor. 4:12).

In reflecting upon the New Testament data concerning the imitation of Christ it is impossible to pass by the several pas-

sages in which is broached conformity to Christ. Do not these
passages create the impression that bare imitation, pure copy
work, is Scriptural after all? Does not such conformity imply
an analogy between the life of believers and that of Christ —
even an identity of the one to the other? And does not the
Bible confirm this idea by saying that Christ dwells in the
hearts of believers (Eph. 3:17)? Listen to Paul: "It is no
longer I that live but Christ liveth in me" (Gal. 2:20). Is
not this a mysticism completely in line with the thirteenth century imitation of Christ?

Undeniably true it is that the New Testament enlarges again
and again on the vital fellowship existing between believers and
Christ — fellowship issuing in conformity. The following passages illustrate this point.

"My little children, of whom I am again in travail until
Christ be formed in you" (Gal. 4:19).

"For whom he foreknew, he also foreordained to be conformed to the image of his Son" (Rom. 8:29).

"Who shall fashion anew the body of our humiliation, that
it may be conformed to the body of his glory" (Phil. 3:21).

The eschatological prospect, though also presented in these
passages, does not preclude a conformity to Christ in this
dispensation. That is evident in the passage from Galatians,
where Paul speaks of the form of Christ. The entire epistle is
full of warnings that the Galatians must not allow themselves
to be bewitched by anything not proceeding from the freedom
they have in Christ. Paul is anxious lest he has bestowed labor
upon them in vain (Gal. 4:11), for their faith has been upset
by a travesty of the Gospel (Gal. 1:7). Upon the heads of its
propagators Paul invokes a frightening Anathema, because by
them the glad tidings of the grace of Christ are being under-
mined. These Galatians must be under an evil spell, since
before their very eyes Christ has been plainly portrayed as crucified. Their confusion is actually a relapse from faith into the
works of the law. They have been baptized into Christ and

THE IMITATION OF CHRIST   157

have put on Christ (Gal. 3:27) and now. . .they seem to be floundering still like little children. Paul has but one purpose in writing the epistle: to set the Galatians straight. And their return is described as Christ being formed in them. Paul wishes to lead them out of the labyrinthine coils of the law and into the open air of God's grace. If they live in unswerving attachment to the grace of Christ, then Christ is formed in them; that is, Christ becomes visible through the abundance of his grace. The Galatians must be so filled with Christ that they bear his very image and he alone becomes visible. For their salvation and life they depend on him alone.

These words about Christ being formed in the believers of Galatia are in complete harmony with Paul's teaching concerning faith and being partakers of the grace of Christ. No new element is added. And that is always the case wherever there is mention of conformity to Christ. The fact that Christ lives in the believer is not a separate, mystical category beside the life of faith. Some day the full glory of Christ will be revealed in the life of believers; but now already there is a renewal of life through fellowship with Christ and through his Spirit (II Cor. 3:18). "Where the Spirit of the Lord is, there is liberty" and we are transformed from glory to glory, a process which practically coincides with that of sanctification. This progress in faith is increasing attachment to Christ and his grace.

Consonant with this idea is what Paul says in Philippians 3. Here he speaks of knowing Christ, and the power of his resurrection, and the fellowship of his sufferings; and here, in connection with knowing Christ, he mentions being conformed unto his death (Phil. 3:10). In this fellowship with Christ he presses on to perfection because he has been laid hold on by Christ (Phil. 3:12). Always it is a fellowship founded on the expiatory suffering of Christ.

This fellowship is fellowship with his grace. The believer enjoying this fellowship is free: free before Christ and his holy

Spirit. He who has become united with him in the likeness of his death will be also in the likeness of his resurrection (Rom. 6:5). Thus Christ lives in his own and is formed in them. Since Christ has been raised from the dead and death has no more dominion over them, they should count themselves to be dead to sin but alive unto God in Christ Jesus (Rom. 6:9-11). And so Paul appeals to them to be transformed by the renewing of their minds and not to be fashioned according to this world (Rom. 12:2). For conformity to (the scheme of) this world is the inversion of conformity to Christ. Paul beseeches believers, by the mercies of God, to abhor conformity to the world.

Albert Schweitzer, who studied the relation between the doctrine of justification by faith and the doctrine of being mystically united with Christ, arrived at the conclusion that the one is ancillary to the other.[7] This conception is in effect a denial of the depth of Paul's view of justification by faith — a doctrine completely oriented toward fellowship with Christ. Schweitzer is compelled to say that Paul cannot logically, on the basis of justification by faith, arrive at any kind of ethics. This conclusion is utterly at variance with the epistles to the Romans and the Galatians. For Paul it is precisely this being in Christ, being crucified, dead, buried, and risen with Christ, which constitutes the riches of justification by faith and for him it is precisely this conformity which enables believers once again to live persuant to these riches and hence not conformably to the scheme of this world. Having reminded his readers in Romans 12 of the mercies of God, he goes on to besiege them with the most concrete admonitions.

The history of the imitation of Christ is a web woven by the play and interplay of reactionary motifs. The motif of the Atonement alternated with that of the Imitation and people complained reciprocally that either the Atonement or the

7. Albert Schweitzer, *Die Mystik des Apostels Paulus*, 1930, pages 207, 220.

Imitation failed to come into its own. Frequently they thought they could best fight the unscriptural imitation by contrasting Christ as Mediator with Christ as Example; the result again was a lapse into onesided emphasis on the Example.

It is possible to clear up the confusion only if one is willing to recognize the fact that, according to the testimony of the entire New Testament, the imitation of Christ is founded on the Atonement. There is absolutely no tension between being reminded of the past (the Atonement) and pressing to the future. In the message of Atonement lies the blueprint for the future. The Atonement and the imitation of Christ are related as a spring to a well and this true imitation of Christ may and must be a leitmotif in the preaching of the church: preaching based on the premise that God was in Christ reconciling the world unto himself (II Cor. 5:19).

One of the most radical conceptions of the imitation of Christ has centered around the law of love. And central in this view was the contrast between law and love. Love as universal principle was understood to exclude justice. Obviously this notion originates in anything but the true imitation of Christ. Conformity to Christ does not consist in isolated human love but in a love which flows from the cross of Atonement upon which God made publicly manifest both his love and his justice.

In the true imitation of Christ it is impossible to celebrate love to the exclusion of justice. Love does exclude the perverted human insistence on one's "rights," which is the opposite of self-denial and which has no eye for the justice and mercy of God; but though this kind of "justice" has no place in the kingdom of God the holiness of God's justice abides. The cross of Christ is precisely a revelation of God's justice. The imitation of Christ as based on the Atonement is also too full of penitence to be subversive of this justice. It is instructive to see how Paul, in Romans 13, after discussing the necessity of government, tribute, custom, and respect for authority,

160 FAITH AND SANCTIFICATION

can just shift to this admonition: "Owe no man anything, save to love one another: for he that loveth his neighbor hath fulfilled the law" (Rom. 13:8). There is a close connection between the love "that worketh no ill to his neighbor" (Rom. 13:10) and the recognition of government, which is a terror to the evildoer (Rom. 13:3).

This is not the place to discuss all the questions that have recently come up in this connection.[8] It is sufficient to say that the Scriptures never indicate any kind of tension between the reconciling act of God in Christ and living by the ordinances of God in this world. If the true imitation of Christ is a revelation of gratitude and hence of having part in the mercy of God, then it will become evident that the believer is not his own, but belongs to God who sways the scepter over his entire life.

The imitation of Christ can therefore never consist in the seclusion of prayer and meditation; instead it takes us into the broad daylight of commonplace affairs. "I pray not that thou shouldest take them from the world, but that thou shouldest keep them from the evil one" (John 17:15). Their only danger is that they will fall in the clutches of the Evil One, and from this danger Christ would have them preserved. In this preservation the imitation fulfills itself as a result of the grace of God who delivered us out of the power of darkness and transferred us into the kingdom of the Son of his love (Col. 1:13-14) and causes us to live as sons of light (I Thess. 5:5). This is the light that radiates from those who follow in the steps of the Master by whose stripes they are healed.

---

8. See Karl Barth, *Rechtfertigung und Recht,* and Emil Brunner, *Gerechtigkeit,* pages 247ff.

Sanctification and Law

CHAPTER VIII

Sanctification and Law

GOOD WORKS, according to Lord's Day 33 of the Heidelberg Catechism, are only those which are done from true faith, to the glory of God, *and according to his law.* Not that these items afford us three independent criteria by which to evaluate good works; for it is clear that true faith cannot but be focussed upon the glory of God and govern itself according to his law. The answer of the Catechism, we may say, has three facets.

The expression "according to the law of God" has been the occasion of much debate. There was always a consensus that good works should be done from true faith and to the glory of God but conformity to the law seemed to be an extraneous element in this description. In any case the expression is superfluous, said some of the disputants, for the designation "from true faith" is sufficient. The additional requirement of conformity to the law will only douse the spontaneity of faith; and the beautiful harmony existing between faith and sanctification will only be disturbed by bringing in the law. Antinomianism understood at least this much that by faith we are under grace and not under law (Rom. 6:14).

Is not the believer free from the law and does not the church live spontaneously in the freedom which it has through the Holy Spirit in Christ Jesus? Why bring up the question of norms under these circumstances?

Naturally, since justification by faith had been joyfully rediscovered by the Reformation as the heart of the biblical message and since for that reason the revolt against Rome was a revolt against justification by the works of the law, it was inevitable that questions should be raised as to the function of the law in the life of believers.

Luther, as we have seen elsewhere, was accused in his day of Antinomianism. The charge was not valid as is evident from Luther's own conflict with Antinomianism — particularly in his opposition to Agricola. Agricola clashed both with Luther and Melanchthon in his views of the law. The issue was not so much the significance of the law for the believer as the necessity of preaching the law of God to the unconverted in order to lead them to repentance. Melanchthon warned against the indiscriminate proclamation of grace and taught that preachers should solemnly insist upon obedience to the law, in order thus to shame the sinner and lead him to faith.

In the teeth of this, Agricola asserted that man can believe only in response to the preaching of the Gospel and accused Melanchthon of a Romanistic perversion of the evangelical doctrines. When later he entered the lists also against Luther he acted on the conviction that he was championing the pure preaching of grace in opposition to all legalism and that he understood the Reformation doctrines with greater penetration than did either Luther or Melanchthon. Whereas the preaching of the law can lead only to despair, true repentance must be produced by the Gospel. His view of the law, felt Agricola, flowed naturally from the free grace of God. Nothing precedes this freedom and nothing, not even repentance, precedes faith. The law, to the recipients of grace at least, is of no further value. "The decalogue belongs in the townhall, not on the pulpit. All who consort with Moses will eventually sell out to the devil. Let Moses be hanged!" (An Galgen mit Mose!) Against this devastating assessment of the decalogue Luther brought all his batteries into play. Convinced though he was of the sovereignty of God's grace and of our inability to be justified by the works of the law, he nonetheless held the law in high esteem and spoke of its threefold intent:

to maintain external order, to induce sinners to recognize their guilt, and to direct the life of believers.

This last function of the law has been the subject of extended debate. The problem, briefly stated, was: How can one recognize this use of the law and still do justice to the free grace of God by which the believer is absolved from the law? The problem is the more interesting since around it has been construed a contrast between Lutherans and Calvinists. Calvinists, despite their adherence to Sola-fide, have made so much of the law, it is said, that for them everything still depends on obedience to the law. On this basis life is again forced into a strait jacket. The Gospel has meaning only in re-opening the narrow gate of painstaking conformity to the law. Even the Heidelberg Catechism seems to pander to this rigorism: does it not speak of good works which *must* be done (Lord's Day 32) and does it not, by such language, put a damper on the spontaneous works of faith and love?

The Lutherans, on the other hand, though they do not deny the significance of the law for believers, refuse to speak of the requirements of the law, since all requirements have been met by Christ. Believers are prompted by love, which enables them of their own accord to do good. Believers, on the Lutheran view, are concerned with the law only to the extent that the old man in them is still unsubdued by the Holy Spirit. Real incentives to good works, however, are from within. Faith and love are independent sources of spontaneous activity. The law no longer hovers over the head of the believer as an alien power but enters into his inmost. Insofar as sin is still present in him, the external law can serve as love — a love which is its own norm and furnishes its own momentum — the believer, to the extent that he really believes, is elevated above the law.[1]

If it were our intention to write a historical analysis of the Reformation, we would first of all point out how, in regard

---

1. This is the view of Schneckenburger.

both to Lutheranism and to Calvinism, the preceding description is a caricature. It is conditioned from beginning to end by an untenable though traditional view of the Reformation and cannot be taken seriously. The point that interests us is the tension here indicated between the spontaneity of faith and the rule of law; between a partial and negative function of the law and a positive function throughout the life of the believer.

The law of God in the life of believers, according to the Reformed view, is definitely not an external force opposed to a spontaneous faith or a spontaneous love. Lord's Day 24 makes it plain that it is inevitable that those who are implanted into Christ by a true faith should bring forth fruits of thankfulness. Reformed theologians distinguished not between spontaneity and law but between spontaneity and compulsion.

Calvin brings this out with great clarity in his discussion of the third use of the law. He talks about the faithful "in whose hearts the Spirit of God already lives and reigns," and in whose hearts the law of God is inscribed by the finger of God so that they are inclined by the direction of the Spirit to obey him; these, says Calvin, "find the law an excellent instrument to give them, from day to day, a better and more certain understanding of the divine will to which they aspire, and to confirm them in the knowledge of it. As, though a servant be already influenced by the strongest desire of gaining the approbation of his master, yet it is necessary for him carefully to inquire and observe the orders of his master, in order to conform to them."[2] Any compulsion, because it is a threat to the voluntary action originating in the gracious work of the Spirit is here excluded. For Calvin, the desire to obey is directed, without fear of clashing, toward the law of God.

The Old Testament encomiums on the law show us "the great advantage derived, through the Divine teaching, from the reading of the law, by those whom God inspires with an inward promptitude to obedience. And he (the Psalmist)

---

2. John Calvin, *Institutes*, II, VII, 12.

adverts not only to the precepts but to *the promise of grace annexed to their performance, which alone causes that which is bitter to become sweet.*"

Calvin evidently believes that the inward promptitude inspired by the Holy Spirit, rather than drawing the believer away from the law, inclines him to listen to the commandment of God and makes him crave a better understanding of the divine will. Faith and love and law, to Calvin, are allies. To reject Moses is to entertain a "profane opinion." Calvin denies that the law "exercises toward us the part of a rigorous exactor," but it rather "shows us a goal, to aim at which, during the whole of our lives, would be equally conducive to our interest and consistent with our duty."[4] Hence the law is not at all in conflict with inward spontaneity; it is not a tyrant suppressing all voluntary desires.

Calvin stresses that the words "I am the Lord thy God, who brought thee out of the land of Egypt, out of the house of bondage" must be considered as a preface to the whole law.[5] "He exhibits a promise of grace, to allure them by its charms to the pursuit of holiness. He reminds the Israelites of his favour, to convict them of ingratitude if they do not conduct themselves in a manner correspondent to his goodness." One might here expect the phrase "in a manner correspondent to his law"; but Calvin, by writing "to his goodness," indicates that the law is indissolubly wedded to the salvation of God and to faith which must, in response to the favors of God, adapt itself to his commandments. To stress the third use of the law is not, of course, exempt from the danger of legalism. This danger becomes immediately acute if one assigns independent significance to the law as regulator of the believer's life and abstracts this law from a responsive gratitude to God for being brought out of the house of bondage. But these

3. *Ibid.,* II, VII, 12.
4. *Ibid.,* II, VII, 13.
5. *Ibid.,* II, VIII, 13.

quite un-imaginary dangers cannot remove an iota or tittle from the fact that Reformed theology, and Calvin in particular, taught that it is precisely a free and spontaneous love which leads the believer to acknowledge the commandments of God.

Granting for the sake of argument that the pivotal difference between Luther and Calvin was that the one restricted the application of the law to the residual evil in man's heart whereas the other viewed the law as over-arching the whole of man's life, it is evident that this difference must also affect their respective views of grace. Actually there is no such difference; all one can say is that a somewhat varying emphasis on the function of the law has had some influence on the subsequent relationship between Lutheranism and Calvinism. Laying aside this historical question, however, we must point out that one may never resort to a separation of the believer as regenerate man, who is now above law, from the old man who is still under its jurisdiction. A full-fledged acknowledgement of the third use of the law, rather than being the offspring of a legalistic orientation, issues from the benefaction of grace which liberates man from a precarious autonomy and places him under the direction of God's holy commandments.

The essential question which has occupied us until now is whether the believer, because he is "under grace," has no further truck with the law. This question, which played a major role in the history of the church, came up in these latter days, tricked out in a relatively new guise, in the ethics of Emil Brunner.

Brunner's arch-contention with anything that smacks of legalism has led him to the distinction — it may be considered the core of his ethics — between law and commandment (Gesetz und Gebot). He did not, from his antipathy to legalism, embrace Antinomianism; for he knew too well the universal rule of law in the life of men. Life could not continue without natural, social, judicial, and moral laws. It is even correct to say that God places us "under law" in order to make life possible.[6] But this law is not the real thing; it is not, essentially, the will of God. Through this law God upholds human life but there is too much of compulsion in it to make it the actual will of God. Compulsion can never be his motive.

"There arises, also for the believer, this remarkable situation that, out of loyalty to God, he has to obey the law, although it does not absolutely express the will of God."[7] The law is but an oblique expression of the will of God and cannot therefore exact unconditional obedience. Whoever teaches that the law requires absolute obedience has identified the law with the actual will of God and has lapsed into a legalistic relationship to God. This nomism can be circumvented only by making the law provisional: a structural support to the life of love.

Final and unconditional obedience can be offered only to the real Will of God and to his actual commandment. In order that the listening ear may hear the Voice that may not go unheeded it is necessary for the believer to break through the outer shell of the law. God's commandments are never general and can never be distilled in external prescriptions; it comes to us in the individual, concrete situation as "God's hint for the Moment."[8] The believer cannot be prompted by an abstract law but only by the voice of God which urges him to make a decision.

All this arises from Brunner's idea that an imperative "Thou-shalt" is incompatible with spontaneous love. "For the good that I do, since I do it under compulsion, I do not freely and voluntarily and it is therefore not a true good."

---

6. Emil Brunner, *Das Gebot und die Ordnungen*, 1932, pages 124ff.
7. *Ibid.*, page 126.
8. Emil Brunner, *Gott und Mensch*, page 38.

The "Thou-shalt" form indicates that immediate unity with the divine will has been lost.

The law, the "Thou-shalt," says Brunner, is impersonal, external, and schematic. Not till the God-man relationship becomes personal in faith and love does obedience take the place of mere legality; then the iron ring of legalism is crushed and the law no longer stands forbiddingly between us and God. The believer takes off the hand-cuffs of the law and hence from all confining schematisms which denature the commandments of God into external legality, that is, into verbal prescriptions or ethical ideals. Love is then through with the law.

In spite of his quarrel with legality, Brunner does not wish to fall a prey to Antinomianism. He believes that the law may still have an "indicative" function in the life of believers and he wishes, even more clearly than Luther, to express this third use of the law. Calvin, says Brunner, had to rap Luther's knuckles on this point, for, though Luther recognized the third use of the law, he did not do much with it. But even Calvin did not entirely succeed in steering clear of the cliffs of legality.[9]

It is not hard to understand Brunner's concern. He consents to the third use of the law but gives it a twist of his own to elude a menacing legalism. He wishes to bring out that, in a state of reconciliation to God, the believer is not a slave, subject to an imperious master, but a servant whose yoke is easy and whose burden is light. He wishes to deal a death-blow to nomism and draw attention to the law as a finger-post. Actually, Brunner knows only the contrast between external law and "being in love." It is practically impossible for him, on the basis of this "being in love," to get back to the law. The life of the believer is divorced from any "Thou-shalt" and

9. Emil Brunner, *Das Gebot und die Ordnungen,* page 585.

beyond the law.[10] It is a life lived completely out of the fount of grace.

Anyone who burns all bridges behind him in this fashion is bound either to take a header into the abyss of Antinomianism or, at the last moment, to spy around for a way back. Brunner prefers to spy around. The atmosphere "beyond the law" gets too rare for him and so he begins to speak about "a law without legality, law interpreted by a faith which knows the grace of God." He cannot do without a law directing us to our neighbor, a law "behind which stands a loving God."[11]

At this point Brunner should have abandoned his distinction between law and commandment and directed his shafts only against the legalistic perversion of the law. He retains the distinction, however, and allows it to play a vast role in a variety of places. Far from confining his operations to a number of incidental ordinances, declaring them to be law — indirect, unreal will of God — he also reduces the ten commandments to this status, that is, "insofar as they are understood as law."

On the one hand, Brunner proceeds on the assumption that there is but one commandment, namely the first: I am thy God. Thou shalt have no other gods before me. This commandment is a call to faith and love. "Really to love him means also to consent to his love: that is faith and the fulfilment of the first commandment. We have no other commandment but this."[12] But on the other hand there is still the nettling fact of theft, adultery, and lying. They, too, are a solid part of the decalogue. If love be "occasionalistic," free from any sort of predetermination, how can it express itself in concrete commandments? Brunner's reply is that the commandments are "testimonies of the Covenant," "testimonies of Revelation." They are "the God-given examples of what

10. *Ibid.*, page 162.
11. *Ibid.*, page 68.
12. *Ibid.*, page 117

his will, of what love means in the concrete situations of life."
They are "paradigms of love."[12]

Brunner is manifestly afraid of the logical deductions of a
casuistry which would spawn a variety of stipulations divorced
from love.   Hence he dubs also the ten commandments as
"law"; but exactly in the appended provision "insofar as they
are understood as law" does the inner contradiction of his
position appear.   He evidently struggles not against the law
but against a misconception of the law.   It simply does not do
to freight the ten commandments with a legalistic distortion
of these commandments in order then to contrast this "law"
with the actual commandment of God.   Fear of legalism, in
Brunner's thinking, has led him to a completely unnecessary
distinction between commandment and law and to the eleva-
tion of the one above the other.   This dualism of commandment and law dominates Brunner's entire ethics. It leads him,
finally, to deny that the believer is wholly subject to the commandment of God.   Brunner's dichotomy is unknown to the
Scriptures.   The Bible presents the law of God in the context of God's electing grace.   A violation of the law is therefore a sin against grace; and to transgress the law is to leave
the path of love.   The ten commandments are indeed forms of
the commandment of love; but one may not sever these paradigms from the law of God.   If man thus puts asunder what
God has joined together, he is playing fast and loose with his
law and cannot but regard it as an outer incrustation to be
blasted by love.

It is important to notice that the opposites to which Brunner draws attention — law and love — are opposites only to
a mind with a warped view of the law.   Such a mind dreams
of the law as something alien, dreary, austere, and never as
the inseparable associate of the grace of God.   What Brunner
calls law, we might characterize as the ten commandments
without the prefaced comfort of "I am the Lord thy God, who

13. *Ibid.*, page 119.

has led thee out of the land of Egypt, out of the house of bondage." Strip the context of grace away, however, and the law becomes unintelligible. For it is not the law which must be removed if man is to gain contact with the actual will of God but it is man's pride which must be exploded if he is to understand the law of God. This very problem already assumed the most troublesome forms among the people of Israel. Having abstracted the law from divine mercy, the Jews were bound to arrive at works-righteousness. But when the eye of faith is riveted upon the grace of God and the God of grace has become our God, then his law is as the voice of the Shepherd to his sheep.

Brunner's contrast between "Thou-shalt" and "being in love," between *Sollen* and *Sein,* is untenable precisely because this *Sein* cannot do without the aid of the *Sollen,* no more than sheep can dispense with the staff of the shepherd. And the sheep of the Shepherd exclaim: "Thy rod and thy staff, they comfort us." The law is a gift of grace.

The yeast of sin and unbelief throws a froth of false assumptions round the law, but these false assumptions may never be thought of as arising from the law itself. The law is enthroned above these assumptions and condemns them because they always tend to pull grace and law and sanctification completely out of joint.

The history of the people of Israel is a drama whose leitmotif is the danger besetting him who misconceives the law. The Gospel nowhere militates against the law but it does trample all over the nomistic interpretations given to the law by the Jews. It always insists that love is the fulfilment of the law (Rom. 13:10) and never that the believers are raised above it. Paul waged his war, too, against the Jewish abstraction of the law by which it was made a doorway to salvation. The careless spectator may imagine that Paul's quarrel is with the law, and Antinomians have always happily hunted in Paul's writings for quotations. Did he not speak of being dead to the law (Gal. 2:19) and of Christ who redeemed them that were under the law (Gal. 4:5)? But it cannot be denied that Paul wishes only to dissociate himself from the law as a way of salvation in the Jewish or Judaistic sense. The law may never be set side by side with or take the place of the Gospel.

Words often quoted in the debate concerning the significance of the law are those of Christ: "Think not that I came to destroy the law or the prophets: I came not to destroy but to fulfil" (Matt. 5:17). Matthew 5 is one grand proof that Jesus, in his public ministry, refused to depreciate the law. All he aims at is fulfilment. And this fulfilment is not merely to provide a prophetic illustration of the purpose of the law but it is the actual Messianic fulfilment by which he attained salvation for man. In this fulfilment, however, is contained such illumination of the law as condemns the externalization of the law by the Pharisees. Not that the significance of Matthew 5 is exhausted by saying that Christ came, in opposition to the rabbinical exposition of the law, to disclose its true intent; nevertheless this purpose is integral with Christ's messianic mission. For in order rightly to understand Christ's fulfilment of the law it is imperative to see which law he fulfilled: the law as fancied by the Pharisees or the law as intended by God.

Paul also was persistently at odds with the Judaistic abuse of the law. Were he in opposition to the law itself, he could not in so facile a fashion shift from preaching the righteousness of faith to pointing out the necessity of fulfilling the law. This shift, rather than taking him onto new ground, is entirely consistent. For this reason — namely that his quarrel is not with the law itself — he places those that are of Christ Jesus and who "have crucified the flesh with the passions and the lusts thereof" (Gal. 5:24) under the dominion of Christ and binds each of them to his neighbor: "Bear ye one another's burdens, and so fulfill the law of Christ" (Gal. 6:2).

For this reason he is able to sprinkle this epistle with admonitions, although he explicitly says he will not glory in anything but the cross of Jesus Christ (Gal. 6:14), as well as to close with a benediction: "The grace of our Lord Jesus Christ be with your spirit" (Gal. 6:18). The flail of admonition is in the hands of a gracious God. For this reason, too, Paul can say that faith does not undermine the law. "God forbid: nay, we establish the law" (Rom. 3:31). This is one of the most remarkable utterances of Paul, for he has just finished saying that "man is justified by faith apart from the works of the law" (Rom. 3:28). There it is: The righteousness of Christ, appropriable by faith outside of the works of the law; by the justification of the ungodly (Rom. 4:5) the delicately geared systems of nomistic religion are once for all shunted aside and declared ineffectual. And in token of this fact the law is established. Not, surreptitiously, by giving it some lackey's job in rearing the structure of righteousness but by opening the eyes of men to its true function. The believer no longer tries to sail heavenwards on clouds of self-righteousness. Having found anchorage in the righteousness of Christ, he has every reason to render obedience to God's laws. In this new obedience the law receives again its original function, a function no longer conceivable in abstraction from the grace of God. For now the commandments are to the believer the gracious guidance of the Savior-God.

Hence Paul can say without a qualm that he is "under law to Christ" (I Cor. 9:21). For him there is no terror in the word "law," nor any tension between being under law and belonging to Christ. He explicitly denies that he is free from the law of God, although to the Jews who keep the Mosaic law he says that he is not under the law. The whole problem of law is solved for Paul — through the righteousness of faith — by this being under the law of God which is the law of Christ. All the anxieties of those who agonize for holiness outside of Christ evaporate in the believer's celebration of the law (compare Rom. 7:22). In Christ alone this joy is real. In Christ alone the believer gratefully bows his head beneath the scepter of God. It is no wonder that Paul, who is under the law of Christ, is eager to win others.

Released from the law, delighting in the law. Paul can speak of the fulfilment of the law by believers to believers: "Through love be servants one to another. For the whole law is fulfilled in one word, even in this: Thou shalt love thy neighbor as thyself" (Gal. 5:13, 14) and "he that loveth his neighbor hath fulfilled the law" (Rom. 13:8). Indeed, faith does not oust the law from its original position. How its function has changed from its former status under the pharisaic regime! From being a curse it has become a canon of gratitude.

*　　*　　*

One of the most central problems touching the relationship of believers to the law is that of *heteronomy*. This heteronomy, because it concerns the law of another (heteros) and hence seems to have something external and alien in it, was widely opposed in the past. In the ethics of many there was a plea for the autonomy of the moral subject over against this heteronomy: should he not offer obedience only to the law emerging from within?

For the life of believers this vast tissue of questions concerning heteronomy and autonomy ceases to be important. Autonomy, at least, is no longer possible under the administration of the Gospel. The Atonement brought release from the self-determination of sin. The entire life of believers is now subject to the will of Another in genuine heteronomy, not as an oppressive menace to burgeoning life but as the sustaining statutory rule of the Other. It is essential that God's law is imposed from without. Now it comes to man as a threat to his autonomy, nullifies this autonomy, and rids him of its illusions. It would never issue forth from the depths of his own heart. The Scriptures do speak of the law as engraved in the heart of man but this God-given readiness to conform to the law of God by no means annuls its heteronomous nature. For it — this heteronomous nature of the law — is completely determined by its being inseparable from the Lawgiver. The law of God is not spread over this world like a net which can be considered by itself; it is the living God who issues that law so that no one can be aware of it without coming in contact with God himself. Therefore the law of God was of such great significance to the people of Israel. Through that law the Lord himself, in all his holiness, approached his people with love and grace. Rightly to understand the Lord is therefore to be docile; and the docile child does not dread his law. To such a child, as to the psalmist who composed Psalm 119, the law is the subject of never-ending litanies.

All Scriptural admonition, because it comes ultimately from the God of the Covenant, bears the impress of his environing protection (Proverbs 6). In this matter God's Revelation is pellucid: "Yet I am Jehovah thy God from the land of Egypt; and thou shalt know no god but me, and besides me there is no saviour. I did know thee in the wilderness" (Hosea 13:4, 5). Again and again this ethnogenic event, this evidence of God's elective love, is played back to the people of Israel from the record of history. The book of Deuteronomy is imbued with this motif: since the Lord has loved them they are to honor his commandments. This heteronomy originates in his grace; and therefore it is not the law which compels, but the urgency of his love which impels the people to show a ready compliance.

To serve other gods is to them a treacherous snare (Deut. 7:16) by which they are snatched out of the range of his grace. The sufferings of this people, too, must be viewed in the light of this relationship: "As a man chasteneth his son, so Jehovah thy God chasteneth thee" (Deut. 8:5). A failure to see the unique relationship existing between God and his people results inevitably in a failure to sense the true character of the law.

The history of the people of Israel has frequently underlined this failure. This people thought it understood, fulfilled, and honored the law but it could not, because it failed to understand the repeated reminder of its remarkable exit from the house of bondage and of God's sacred property rights. All instruction in the law is primarily instruction in the way God deals with his people. Disruption of sacred ties is possible only by a denial of the law as the rule of God's gracious covenant. It is of relatively little moment whether this disruption occurs by open revolt or by the substitution of self-righteousness.

Covenant obligations were not obligations to an abstract law but to him who led his people out of Egypt. And the sin of the people, in Hosea's time for instance, was the sin of not requiting God's covenant love. In the midst of serious indictments Hosea stops to remind the people of "the days of her youth" when she sang praises coming out of Egypt (Hosea 2:15). When the valley of Achor shall have become a door of hope, after Israel's dismal alienation from her maker (Hosea 8:14), she, the affianced of the Lord, shall know him (Hosea 2:20).

The moment this perspective is lost, the law withers into a moral code and the way is open to a senseless cult, equally abhorrent to God's prophets as Israel's national pride. By way of this descending spiral the people at length reached its utmost desolation in exile. This people thought of the law as its own property and not as God's. It absolutized the law and by this token, strange though this may sound, made it, religiously speaking, relative. At last in Pharisaism the secret of the chosen people is lost — swallowed up by a devouring casuistic legalism. It seemed that in Pharisaism all the essentials of the law were preserved: its holy character, its inviolable authority, and the blessing which rewards its fulfilment. Actually everything is changed: the law of God has been turned into a falsehood and now resembles a mere rule, a flower cut off from its stem and caught in an irreversible process of decay. The misshapen thing that used to be the law has lost its authority, the authority of grace, and its blessing is changed into a curse. For the people of Israel as well as for later Jewry the law retained its key-position, but the key can no longer open the doors of the Kingdom. Even if the law should be viewed as pre-existent, eternal, and as operative at the creation of the world, its depth and its joyful exuberance are no more; if anything remains of it at all it is in the hideous parody of pharisaic pride over moralistic achievements.

In head-on collision with this decadent heteronomy stand the laws by which the living God places human life beneath the scepter of his grace. No greater contrast is conceivable than that between the life lived in the radiance of God's gracious laws and the life lived in the darkness of works-righteousness. The Scriptural substructure of the rule of God's law is his grace, the source of Israel's holiness. Therefore its being under the law was not an addition foreign to its being under grace but merely the demand to live conformably to the riches of this grace. This demand is no less serious than it would be on a moralistic basis. It is a call to be living branches of the Vine.

*   *   *

One can speak variously of the Christian life. It may be viewed in terms of following Christ and living in conformity to his will. It may also be viewed in terms of living in freedom. Being bound to the law of God has never been more profoundly described than in the term "Christian liberty."

People have often smiled their pitying smile when it was said that the greatest freedom consists in the strictest subjection to law. Indeed, in a morally dislocated world it is quite conceivable that such a characterization should no longer strike a responsive chord. But the Gospel makes plain the connection between being free and being bound. To be accurate, we should say that freedom and bondage are co-extensive, identical: and this identity is rooted in Jesus Christ who is the Lord of life.

"If therefore the Son shall make you free, ye shall be free indeed" (John 8:36). In these few words is summarized the entire New Testament teaching concerning the freedom of believers. And this liberty is not the product of human craving and human action but a condition brought about by a divine miracle. It is unique: unsolicited by man, gratuitously given by God.

The New Testament treats of this act of Christ in varied language. Paul uses the word "redemption," paying a ransom in order to free the sinner from the curse of the law (Gal. 3:13). By becoming a curse for us, Christ redeemed those that are under the law in order that they may receive the adoption (Gal. 4:5). Obviously this redemption is an awesome transaction by which slaves are granted the freedom of the children of God. The condition of man outside of Christ is always characterized in the New Testament as one of bondage, slavery, subjection to sin. He is under the law: not only subject to the law but subject to its curse. Into this prison-house of death Christ entered as Redeemer and transferred the curse to his cross. Hence the resultant liberty, the condition of being redeemed from the curse, presupposes a condition of utter peonage or bondage, and can be understood only as freedom from this bondage. This freedom has many positive values, for Christ who redeems also reconciles and converts the ex-slaves into children of the Most High.

These two conditions are antipodal. On the one hand, there is the slavery of sin. Christ himself gave expression to this idea when he said: "Everyone that committeth sin is a bond-servant (doulos) of sin" (John 8:34). The condition of bondage exists wherever a man is subjected, body and soul, bag and baggage, to another or to a given power. To commit sin, which seems to be freedom from the law of God, is at bottom only bondage. Sin dictates the terms of a man's life (Rom. 6:19). Man's autonomy is shown to be a mirage; the truth is that he is a peon to iniquity. Then there is liberty: a liberty from the very beginning described as having its greatest riches in bondage to the Liberator. The New Testament does not shrink from using the word *doulos* to characterize either condition. The content of *doulos,* of course, varies radically in its dual application. To be a servant, a *doulos,* to sin is to have a relentless tyrant as master; to be bound as *doulos* to Christ is to have love itself as Master. The terror of the former condition is supplanted by gratitude and willingness in the other.

An imagined autonomy — in reality a definite bondage — has to yield before the new heteronomy instituted by Christ. The horror implicit to many in the word heteronomy is removed by the Other who is Jesus Christ the Liberator-God. This heteronomy is not an attack upon the fortress of man's privacy but rather a shield behind which he may rally throughout his life. The reign referred to, as contrasted with the reign of sin, is that of grace (Rom. 5:21; 6:12).

The liberty of believers, as was intimated, is both negative and positive: it consists in being redeemed *from* and being redeemed *unto.* Once the bond written in ordinances against us has been blotted out, principalities and powers are subdued, despoiled, and disarmed, and concurrently the dead are made alive together with Christ (Col. 2:13-15) so that Paul can say elsewhere that God leads us in triumph in Christ (II Cor. 2:14). This triumph carries with it the death-warrant for every refinement of religious autonomy. All that is left now is the memory of the conquest of Christ and the new commandment implicit in it. Now rules the law of liberty (James 1:25; 2:12); "proof of freedom from the law lies in the consumma-

tion of the law of liberty."[14] What striking evidence this is
of the harmony existing between Paul and James. Their respective idioms may differ, but both testify to the freedom
which is in Jesus Christ. Human life is truly redeemed, restored, and transferred by Christ from the dominion of darkness into the Kingdom of light.

Sanctification and law are inseparable; within their com-
pass moves all of redeemed human life.

Freedom in and through Christ, wherever it exists, is vast-
ly different from any individualistic kind of freedom. Being
free in Christ is synonymous with being his possession. He
is the Lord who has redeemed us, body and soul, from the
power of the devil and, by this means, made us his own pos-
sessions.[15] Thus believers are shaken out of the individualistic isolation in which they imagined themselves free from their
neighbor and in which only their own lives seemed of supreme
importance. The transition from being a slave of sin to being
a servant of Christ is one which thrusts the believer into fellowship with his neighbor.

The freedom of the believer must not be conceived as being
restricted or delimited by his obligations to his neighbor;
precisely in the bond which draws him to his neighbor does
this freedom reveal itself. The essence of freedom in Christ
can come to expression only in Christian fellowship. When
Paul exclaims: "Through love be servants one to another"
(Gal. 5:13) and "he that loveth his neighbor hath fulfilled
the law" (Rom. 13:8), he implies that Christian liberty must
be manifested in service and love. Is not freedom identical
with bondage to Christ and to his law? These relationships
come to the fore especially in Rom. 14 and I Cor. 8. Pre-
dominant in these chapters is the weak-brother motif. Paul's
attitude reveals that believers are to govern themselves, to a
certain extent, in accordance with the dangers besetting the

14. *Kittel's Wörterbuch,* II, 499.
15. *Heidelberg Catechism,* Question 34.

weak brother. Paul knows that in the abstract the believer is permitted to eat things not in themselves unclean. But in the concrete situation the weak brother has to be taken into account. For "if because of meat thy brother is grieved, thou walkest no longer in love" (Rom. 14:15). Warningly Paul adds: "Destroy not with thy meat him for whom Christ died." He certainly does not surrender the weak brother to the whims of the free believer. Instead, he brings out the connection between serving Christ and mutual edification (Rom. 14:19). Bearing the infirmities of the weak is an exercise in following the Example, Christ, who also pleased not himself (Rom. 15:1-3). The same teaching is contained in I Cor. 8. Again Christian liberty is shown to be devoid of individualistic traits. Should this be forgotten, "he that is weak perisheth" as a result of the knowledge of the strong (I Cor. 8:11). To sin thus against the brethren is to sin against Christ (I Cor. 8:12).

On the basis of all this, one should not say that it is optional whether to use one's Christian liberty or not; for the man who abstains from a given thing in order not to offend his brother is also using his Christian liberty. Instead of saying that in a certain situation we do not use our Christian liberty, we should rather say that we manifest that liberty in the act by which we pressure the brother from stumbling. One can speak of not using Christian liberty and refer to the liberty we have to eat or not to eat. In the absence of the weak brother, Christian liberty manifests itself in the option to indulge or not to indulge; in the presence of the weak brother, when this liberty can no longer operate in isolation, it manifests itself in not eating for the sake of this brother.

Not to comply at this point with Paul's teaching would be to abstract one's freedom from the total reality in which it is exercised and thus to sin against Christ. There is no difference between Christian liberty and being "under the law of Christ." Whoever loves his neighbor has fulfilled this law.

Thus the harmonious relation between sanctification and law becomes visible. All legalism is excluded by the orientation of faith operative in sanctification. Luther and Calvin, as we know, opposed Rome in its teaching of justification through love. But we must not think that, by this token, they wished to deprecate love; on the contrary, they sought merely to echo Paul's doctrine of faith working through love.

The moment sanctification is isolated from faith in God's mercy it degenerates into a dreary and unsolaced nomism in which there is no room for the motive of gratitude and responsive love to God.

The golden triad of faith, sanctification, and law, is beautifully interpreted in the Heidelberg Catechism. The decalogue is treated under the heading of Gratitude; but not for a moment do the authors lose sight of the preceding doctrines of Misery and Redemption. The Catechism describes the decalogue as a complex of canons revealing the nature of the people of God as well as the forms in which their life is cast. It expresses this idea in several places. One has to think only of the first and second commandments, of the way God would teach his people,[16] of praising and confessing the holy Name of God,[17] of the glory of God,[18] of hearing Gods' Word and using the sacraments,[19] of submission to divine authority, of duties to one's neighbor and one's enemies,[20] and of preserving oneself as a temple of the Holy Spirit.[21]

Clearly outlined in these few expressions are the contours of the people of God, of a priesthood which lives by faith and is therefore placed under the royal law of liberty. It is surely not by chance that the decalogue begins with this most fundamental commandment: "Thou shalt have no other gods before

16. Question 98.
17. Question 99.
18. Question 101.
19. Question 103.
20. Question 107.
21. Question 109.

me." At the entrance of the heathen land of Canaan was sounded this basic law of Israel's existence: "Hear, O Israel: Jehovah our God is one Jehovah" (Deut. 6:4). That law was to be their great support. He is the only Lord: and therefore the people must love him with all their heart, soul, and might. It is no subtlety of theologians to say that for the church of the Reformation everything depends on a right understanding of the first commandment. The pivotal significance of this commandment also appears from the interpretation of the Catechism.[22] All rays of meaning are gathered together and brought to focus upon the only, true God, whom alone we are to acknowledge, trust, and love. And idolatry is antithetically described as having and devising something on which to trust outside of the one God who revealed himself in Scripture. The first commandment contains the truth which is implicit in Lord's Day 1 concerning the "only comfort in life and death" which consists in being the possession of Jesus Christ.

In the decalogue man's relation to God is forever distinguished from any and every humanitarian ideal of morality and conditioned by faith in God's solacing grace. Without this grace the doctrine of gratitude and grateful devotion to the law of God would totter.

*   *   *

In this connection we must discuss also the Sermon on the Mount. Too often this sermon has been interpreted as a new law, as was done also, we remember, with the imitation of Christ. The Christian life, it was said, is here given an entirely new interpretation; a new complex of laws, announced on the Mount of Beatitudes, is to hold sway over the life of sanctification.

Again we are concerned with the essential relationship between sanctification and law. Since it is impossible here to

---

22. Question 94.

discuss the Sermon itself we shall confine ourselves to what a nomistic interpretation has done with it.

The topic of the Sermon on the Mount is the righteousness that exceeds the righteousness of the scribes and Pharisees. As the Exodus of Israel was the foundation of the decalogue, so communion with Christ is central in the directives of the Sermon. To the disciples Christ says: "Ye are the salt of the earth" (Matt. 5:13), and "Ye are the light of the world" (Matt. 5:14). It is they who must so let their light shine before men that men may see it and glorify the Father. To omit communion with Christ from this Sermon is to reduce it to a law as impracticable as the decalogue would be without antecedent grace.

When Karl Barth sought to undo the nomistic wrappings from the Sermon on the Mount, he ran into the problem of what *is* and what *ought* to be. He pointed out the agreement between the Sermon and the decalogue. The object of the decalogue, he says, is "delimitation." The decalogue defines the area within which the chosen nation must move; an area in which the constitution of the covenant of grace alone is valid. It exhibits a given relationship in which God is to bid and to forbid. What God will command, what his directions will be or appear to be — "that we cannot learn from the ten commandments as such, or from the law as further amplified, but that we must learn from the remaining biblical histories and from those descriptions of concrete obedience for which a particular person is instructed in a particular situation — that we must learn from the direct speech of Moses on the Mount."[23]

According to Barth, the law proclaims who it is that speaks and who they are to whom the law is announced. Not the content of the commandments but the fact of God's speaking and commanding within this given area is the more impor-

---

23. Karl Barth, *Kirchliche Dogmatik* II, 2, page 765.

tant. "To keep the ten commandments means to assume the status indicated and outlined by these commandments."

Clearly, Barth wishes, in his interpretation of the decalogue as "Ortsangabe" — as indicative of relative position — to maintain the priority of divine grace over against all forms of nomistic righteousness. But he stresses the separation of God's people in a manner which leaves the impresssion that "Ortsangabe" is more important than the content of the commandments. There is in fact no inconsistency between the status of God's people and their obligations. The whole idea of the decalogue is to state the duties of these people to whom God said, "I am the Lord thy God." Why should one stress the one element to the exclusion of another? Of course, Barth is plagued by the devil of legalism and now hurls his inkpot at him. To hit him, however, it is not necessary to deny the importance of the actual content of the law. Legalism springs not from over-emphasizing its content but from misconceiving it. Israel failed to see in the law the radiant grace of the Lawgiver; it failed to sound the depths of love and the response of gratitude as the fulfilment of the law.

Barth's interpretation of the Sermon on the Mount is cast in the same anti-nomistic mold. His discussion, though sound in stressing the centrality of Christ and his Kingdom in the Sermon, becomes a disappointing devaluation of its concrete directives. In view of the notorious non-fulfilment of the ten commandments by the people of Israel, it would be "sheer madness,"[24] according to Barth to try to realize the directives of the Sermon. What then is the sense of the Sermon? Merely to expose the incapacity of sinners? No, says Barth. The Sermon is addressed to the sinner as called by Christ. It presents to us the life of the new man as he is in Christ who has perfectly fulfilled the law. Again Barth fears the perverted exegesis which would isolate the Sermon from the Gospel of grace. Man, he says, must take

---

24. Karl Barth, *op. cit.*, page 770.

account of this summary of divine commandments in order that he may be able to hear, really to hear, the ordinances which concern his real life. It is unnecessary to point out the analogy of Barth's view to the distinction, propagated by Brunner, between law and commandment. We reply that it is precisely God's grace, operative in the atonement which provided the ground for gratitude, which gave believers also the law as the concrete expression of the divine will to be the guide for their faith.

In numerous ways, throughout the history of the church, the true relationship between Gospel and Law has been obscured. Two opposite tendencies are apparent: the tendency to make the Gospel into a new law and the tendency to sever the Gospel from the law.

In order to save morality, ethics, human activity, and human responsibility, some thought it necessary to restrict the sovereign grace of God; in order to preserve the purity of the Gospel, others thought it necessary to exclude all influence upon human morality. In this confusion of nomism and antinomianism we should have to, it seems, were it necessary to make a choice, cast our vote for antinomianism which at least champions the sovereignty of grace, whereas nomism champions human dignity and responsibility. But it should not be forgotten that, from a failure to realize that God in his grace calls upon man to serve him, antinomianism is likewise incapable of fully honoring the grace of God. It is obvious by this time that the call to service itself constitutes the riches of grace. Failure to realize this truth is found among those who do wish to honor the grace of God but, because of their antinomianism, must constantly be reminded of the true nature of the law of God. The responsibility of the church is grave indeed. It must preach salvation full and free; and be constantly vigilant against both nomism and antinomianism.

These dangers can be overcome only by a faith that yields itself wholly to the grace of God. If this surrender be genuine there cannot but be an open ear for the voice of the Good Shepherd who says: "My sheep hear my voice, and I know them, and they follow me" (John 10:27).

Now we are in a position to discuss the question of how to formulate the relationship between Law and Gospel. Karl Barth has made a plea for the order "Gospel and Law," although he does not deny that there is something to be said for the traditional order. The problem we are facing is whether priority must be assigned to the law or to the gospel. First of all we must make clear that the intent of the traditional order, "law and gospel" was certainly not to make the gospel dependent on the law. The expression was universally used to indicate that both constitute a part of divine revelation. Moreover, it was understood that law and gospel could not simply be arranged under, or identified with, the divisions of Old and New Testament. The Old Testament is not without gospel and the New Testament is not without law. Nowadays some people speak rather emphatically about "gospel and law." The idea is to bring out that law and gospel belong together and that we cannot understand the law without the gospel; and to underscore the fact that the gospel brings salvation to sinful human beings and that in this process they are called to service and obedience. This connection between gospel and law is taught by Paul in practically every sentence he wrote. Not that the law has no significance for the unbeliever. The Reformation also asserted the function of the law by which sinners are led to repentance. But the central idea was certainly the priority of the gospel — implying that man having the law without the gospel is in a predicament from which he cannot escape. To speak of "gospel and law" may be to give a sound reproduction of "I am the Lord thy God who led thee out of the land of Egypt" which prefaces the ten commandments. In this order is implied that God opens a way — not of righteousness by works — but a way at whose beginning he stands in an act of deliverance. The law makes sense only to the man who has understood this elective love of God and the covenant of grace. In opposition to all the perils attending the believer in his pilgrimage of faith, he must forever repeat: Gospel, grace, and law — these are the essential links. The eternal truth is that the law never stands by itself but can be found only, as under the old Dispensation, in the ark of the Covenant.

Pursuantly to the numerous passages in the New Testament referring to deliverance from the curse of the law, it is possible also to speak of "law and gospel." The gospel is then viewed against the background of the law as a deadly force to all who would be justified by the works of the law. But when we thus view the law as a "presupposition" of the gospel we must mean the law as misunderstood and the gospel as that which stops us from coddling the law as the source of our salvation. Hence neither the formulation "law and gospel" nor that of "gospel and law" ought to be objectionable as long as the core idea — that grace alone is able to place us "under the law" in the full sense of this phrase — is underscored. With this provision in mind we sense that the law was never issued without the gospel and the gospel never announced without the law.

Some, among them Barth, have spoken of the laws as the form of the gospel whose content is grace. We protest against the reduction of the law to this status; by it the law is practically dissolved in the gospel. The gospel indeed precedes the law — "I am thy God" precedes "Thou shalt" — but this priority of grace does not destroy the imperative force of the law.

The Belgic Confession gives beautiful expression to the harmony existing between law and gospel. In Article 24, concerning "Sanctification," it discusses the works "which God has *commanded* in his Word," and in Article 22, concerning "Justification," it glories in Jesus Christ who imputes 'to us all his merits, and so many holy works which he has done for us and in our stead."

Law and grace — a perfect harmony; but law without gospel, or thora without the covenant, must always clash with grace.

The linkage between faith, sanctification, and law, has never been more brilliantly high-lighted than by Paul: "For we are his workmanship, created in Christ Jesus for good works, which God afore prepared that we should walk in them" (Eph. 2:10). It appears that in his reasoning Paul is here pushing to this one goal: that we should walk in good works. This conclusion is the more surprising because the context is exhaustively concerned with the sovereign grace of God in Christ Jesus. The initial point of discussion was the transition from a false faith to the true faith, a transition exclusively founded upon the mercy of God (Eph. 2:4). "For by grace have ye been saved through faith; and that not of yourselves, it is the gift of God; not of works that no man should glory" (Eph. 2:8, 9). At this point Paul brings up the good works of those who are God's workmanship, God's poems, and says, to our amazement, that God prepared these works. The path of good works runs not from man to God, says Paul, but from God to man. Salvation is by grace — good works included.

Obviously, this is something which an autonomous morality can never grasp. Faith, not ethics can assimilate the priority of divine grace even in good works. Calvin, in his commentary on Ephesians, rightly says that all human glorying is excluded because the very order proves "that God is not at all indebted to us for the good works we do." They are taken from his treasury in which they were afore prepared. For "whom he called, them he also justified: whom he justified, them he also glorified." Not that Paul posits the pre-existence of good works but he wishes to make clear that any inclination of the believer to good works originates in the prior preparation of God. The children of God are ready to submit themselves to the holy law of God which is now the rule of their lives. But this readiness is no other than gratitude and this gratitude is itself part of the good works which God afore prepared. Such good works constitute a goal, says Paul: "that we should walk in them." Walking thus in the works afore prepared by God we shall understand the warning "that no man should glory."

The believer, far from being isolated in the process of sanctification, will, if he walks in the good works afore prepared, be a light in the world environing him. This light is not limelight; this sanctification shuns theatrical piety. The more good works are viewed in the light of revelation as afore prepared by God, the more they will be distinguishable from a spurious holiness. This distinction is recurrent in Scripture. Christ speaks of those who have prophesied by his name, and by his name cast out demons and done mighty works; but in reality they were workers of iniquity and Christ has never known them (Matt. 7:22). The warning remains as long as a gross discrepancy between the outside and the inside, between external righteousness and internal hypocrisy, as illustrated by the scribes and Pharisees, prevails.

In true faith the inner and outer aspect of life are harmoniously developed. The law drives the believer out into the world — to his neighbor, to his poor brother and sister (James 2:15), to his enemy, to his brother in prison, to the hungry and thirsty ones; and thrusts him into contact, for good or for ill, with earthly gods, marriage, and civil authority.

The winged words "Love God and do as you like" were intended to place sanctification in the light of spontaneous love. As such this epigram seems to stand on a higher plane than that on which life "under the law is consummated. But at bottom it reveals only one aspect of sanctification: its orientation in love for God. Scripture goes further. It teaches also love for one's neighbor and continually subordinates the human will to the divine commandments.[25] For the law of Christ overarches the whole of the lives belonging to him. This law, though Christ's law, is nonetheless law.

In the bond between faith and sanctification we perceive, no less than in the bond between faith and justification, the pulse-beat of the Gospel. If faith will but lift its blossoms to catch the sunlight of God's grace, the fruit will be a life imbued with holiness.

---

25. "Augustine's 'Love and do as you like' has the value of a challenging epigram, but it can be seriously misleading. It is too much exposed to the danger of a barren sentimentality. At any rate few of the New Testament writers seem to have been content to leave it at that. Most of them spend a good deal of their paper upon quite specific injunctions for Christian conduct in a variety of actual situations" (C. H. Dodd, *The Gospel and the Law of Christ*, page 13).